ROUTLEDGE LIBRARY EDITIONS:
SOVIET POLITICS

I0127956

Volume 20

THE SOVIET SPACE PROGRAMME

THE SOVIET SPACE PROGRAMME

RONALD D. HUMBLE

Routledge
Taylor & Francis Group

LONDON AND NEW YORK

First published in 1988 by Routledge

This edition first published in 2024
by Routledge
4 Park Square, Milton Park, Abingdon, Oxon OX14 4RN

and by Routledge
605 Third Avenue, New York, NY 10158

Routledge is an imprint of the Taylor & Francis Group, an informa business

British Library Cataloguing in Publication Data
A catalogue record for this book is available from the British Library

ISBN: 978-1-032-67165-9 (Set)
ISBN: 978-1-032-67547-3 (Volume 20) (hbk)
ISBN: 978-1-032-67549-7 (Volume 20) (pbk)
ISBN: 978-1-032-67548-0 (Volume 20) (ebk)

DOI: 10.4324/9781032675480

Publisher's Note
The publisher has gone to great lengths to ensure the quality of this reprint but points out that some imperfections in the original copies may be apparent.

Disclaimer
The publisher has made every effort to trace copyright holders and would welcome correspondence from those they have been unable to trace.

Preface to the 2024 Edition
The Soviet Space Programme

When this book was published in 1988 it ended with somewhat grand, and as it turned out inaccurate, expectations on the future of the Soviet space programme. Then in 1989 the Soviet Union began to collapse and all bets were off for what would become essentially the Russian space program. The American space shuttle Space Transportation System (STS) seemed the way of the future and China was still a minor space player. The showcase Soviet Buran space shuttle had only completed a single uncrewed one orbit mission in 1988 before it and its super heavy lift booster Energia, which together had been allocated the lion's share of the Soviet space budget, were abandoned in disarray with the space shuttle itself being destroyed after its storage hangar collapsed in 2002, and follow-on shuttles never being completed. After the fall of the Soviet Union the space sector had almost collapsed and largely survived during the 1990s by creating various foreign commercial joint-ventures to the concern of many Russians who feared that the results of decades of R&D had turned into bargain sales.

My predictions of Soviet space colonies with cosmonauts on the Moon and Mars were not to be, but Russian space efforts would nevertheless persevere, albeit now more often closer to home. When I wrote this book over thirty-five years ago reliable information on the Soviet space programme was scarce and difficult to obtain. Today there is a surplus of data from multiple sources and the challenge is to separate mis- and disinformation from probable fact and to synthesize this into a useful summary that makes sense of their overall programme direction.

As a result of its Soviet design and production bureau heritage, Russia's space sector today is largely descended from these State organizations. The Roscosmos State Corporation provides a coordinating role similar to NASA but is a state enterprise rather than a public non-profit agency, and its establishment was a major part of a 2013 complex reorganization and streamlining of the remnant Soviet space sector. It is responsible for overall space operations, cosmonaut programs and civilian and military aerospace R&D. Its subsidiary Glavkosmos promotes the global marketing of the Russian space programme and manages complex international projects.

However, Roscosmos has often been accused of misspending and financial irregularities to the detriment of overall programme activities. A new National Space Centre in Moscow is to headquarter thousands of employees from Roscosmos and other space related organizations as part of the Technopolis Moscow special economic zone.

The civilian annual space budget in recent years has never been more than several billion or less U.S. dollars, about a tenth of NASA's, but comparisons are difficult due to Russia's special allocations for space infrastructure development, large military space related projects that are often dual-use, and economic purchasing power parity considerations.

RSC Energia is the nation's largest space enterprise and the prime crewed spacecraft contractor (improved Soyuz types for crewed missions and the recent Progress MS robot supply vehicle, and a Universal Spacecraft Configuration for new communications, navigation, remote sensing and servicing satellites). The overall sector has some one hundred firms and perhaps up to a quarter of a million employees although this would also include military space activities.

Other major firms include the Khrunichev State Research and Production Space Center (Proton, Rokot and Angara series launch vehicles as well as space station modules) and the Progress Rocket Space Centre (Soyuz launch vehicle series and satellites), Information Satellite Systems Reshetnev (the major satellite producer including the GLONASS series and communications and research systems), and NPO Lavochkin (Fregat upper stages for large payloads, as well as interplanetary spacecraft).

NPO Energomash is the major rocket engine supplier formed from a major consolidation of various propulsion firms, and produces a large number of designs. Its RD-180 and RD-181 engines have even been adopted under license by the U.S., although the Americans are now developing alternatives, and it has developed new designs such as the RD-191 developed for the recent Angara launch vehicle, and the PDU-99 for the new Sarmat ICBM.

EDB Fakel is a specialist in ion and plasma space propulsion systems which could see increased overall future applications. KB Arsenal, which developed nuclear powered RORSAT ocean reconnaissance satellites in the past, is rumoured to be working on a secretive nuclear powered satellite called Ekipazh that would use plasma electric propulsion and could have multiple applications such as powerful electronic warfare platforms and even space tugs. Russia is developing the 9M730 Burevestnik (SSC-X-9 Skyfall) nuclear powered strategic cruise missile with claimed unlimited range, and while not a space system it is indicative of their continued serious efforts in this propulsion field that could have broad space applications.

In terms of infrastructure, the Baikonur (Tyuratam) Cosmodrome in Kazakhstan continues to be used for Proton, Angara, Zenit, Soyuz, Tsyklon, and Dnepr (converted SS-18 Satan ICBMs) launch vehicles and maintains a busy launch pace although military activities have recently been somewhat minimized. It is the only Cosmodrome from which missions to the International Space Station (ISS) are launched, and it is jointly managed by Roscosmos and the Russian Space Forces, with its lease expiring in 2050. Recent financial and political tensions between Kazakhstan and Russia make it more likely that operations will be moved to the new Vostochny Cosmodrome as soon as possible.

The old Kapustin Yar test range still carries out the occasional military test launch. The European Space Agency's spaceport in French Guiana, Kourou, had been the first Western spaceport to accommodate Russian launches but such cooperation was suspended in 2022 due to sanctions imposed on Russia over the war in Ukraine.

The Plesetsk Cosmodrome is used for the development and launch of the Soyuz series, Cosmos-3M, Tsyklon, Angara, and Rokot (converted RS-18A/SS-19 Stiletto ICBM) launch vehicles, as well as new generation ICBM launch tests, and is particularly well suited for polar and high inclination orbits such as the Molniya orbits.

Sary-Shagan in Kazakhstan, mostly abandoned during the 1990s, now continues with some recent modernization efforts as a ballistic missile defense and directed energy weapons test site, but like Baikonur concerns likely exist over its location. In addition, Russia boasts over fifteen other military missile test and deployment sites that could be used for some space launches.

After some four decades of planning, design and construction, Russia's newest Cosmodrome at Vostochny near the old Svobodny Cosmodrome north of Vladivostok is intended to replace Baikonur. It witnessed its first orbital launch on April 28, 2016, and a number of successful launches have subsequently been made. It is designed for the launch of Angara, Soyuz and future very heavy lift vehicles securely within Russia's own territory, and has specialized launch sites for crewed missions. It is also intended as a massive economic development stimulus for Russia's poorer Far East, but has seen recent numerous financial difficulties and construction delays, with some seeing it as a drain of scarce resources that could have been better applied to other space projects such as those related to planetary exploration.

During the 1990s sea-based launch platforms were explored with US joint-venture partners, but all such deals fell apart due to financial and other difficulties. However, Russia's Shtil three stage vehicle is the first capable of launching satellites to orbit from a submerged submarine.

Of course, much of Russia's space efforts remains linked to military developments and are often dual-use in nature. The Russian Space Forces is their equivalent of the U.S. Space Force and was formed in 2015 by merging the space assets of the Russian Air Force and their Aerospace Defence Forces. It shares much of the Russian space infrastructure with Roscosmos. The Russian Strategic Rocket Forces is a separate military branch that controls all land based ICBMs, medium range missiles and related infrastructure and works closely with the Space Forces and Roscosmos.

The Main Centre for Reconnaissance of the Situation in Space and the Main Centre for Missile Attack Warning near Moscow are headquarters of the Russian Space Forces' space surveillance network including missile early attack warning and overall space object surveillance. The Titov Space Control Centre near Moscow is the primary Russian military and commercial satellite operations centre.

Since Russia's invasion of Ukraine, Roscosmos launched at least sixteen satellites in support of their war effort. Russia currently operates some 24 GLONASS navigation/geolocation satellites, with the GLONASS-M and GLONASS-K series being the most recent models that have accuracies of at least .06 meters. Russia also currently employs the new generation Meridian telecommunications satellites, Kondor-FKA synthetic aperture radar/electro-optical reconnaissance satellites, Liana electronic intelligence satellite system, Repei signals intelligence satellites, and the EKS satellite missile attack early warning system, amongst various others.

For its strategic forces, legacy ICBMs are being removed from service and replaced by new systems such as the RT-2PM2 Topol-M (SS-27 Sickle B) with single or multiple independently targetable reentry vehicle (MIRV) warhead variants including the upgraded RS-24 Yars. Topal-M solid fuel engines were developed at the Soyuz Federal Centre for Dual-Use Technologies and permit a much higher acceleration than most ICBM types as well as a much flatter trajectory and is considered Russia's most accurate ICBM. An intermediate range missile type, the solid fuel RS-26 Rubezh, is to be equipped with MIRVs or hypersonic Avangard glide vehicle nuclear or conventional warheads. Russia claims that Avangard's speed (up to Mach 27) combined with high maneuverability and low altitude trajectories makes it invulnerable to any current ballistic missile defence system.

The key liquid fuelled super heavy RS-28 Sarmat ICBM developed and produced by Roscosmos and its Makeyev Rocket Design Bureau was put into initial service in September 2023, and is intended as an eventual replacement for the R-36M2 Voyevoda (SS-18 Satan) heavy ICBM with an initial production run of at least fifty missiles. With a compressed early launch phase to decrease the likelihood of satellite detection, it is now the world's heaviest ICBM at some 208 tons with an eleven ton payload. Hardened silo based, its payload consists of up to ten to fifteen nuclear armed MIRVs or twenty-four Avangard glide vehicles. Russia claims a single Sarmat, now nicknamed "Satan 2", can devastate an area exceeding the size of France or Texas. Capable of a 35,000 kilometre suborbital flight and a depressed attack trajectory over the South Pole or any direction to North America, this monster missile has potentially provided Russia with a renewed Fractional Orbit Bombardment System (FOBS), a capability that the Soviet Union supposedly gave up by the early 1980s in compliance with the Strategic Arms Limitation Talks II Treaty.

In July 2020, Russia tested a satellite close inspection spacecraft Cosmos 2543 that has anti-satellite (ASAT) potential that was launched from the Cosmos 2542 satellite and undertook maneuvers against a third Russian spacecraft and an American reconnaissance satellite. Cosmos 2543 also released another fast projectile that could be evidence of a space weapon system. In November 2021 Russia tested a direct ascent System A-235 PL19 Nudol ASAT missile against a defunct Cosmos satellite resulting in a large debris field in low earth orbit, their first test of this kind against an actual target. The Nudol system equipped with nuclear and conventional warheads is also being deployed as a ballistic missile defence (BMD) system for key areas such as Moscow and important industrial sites, and can even be used against hypersonic targets. The S-500 Prometey hypersonic surface to air missile also provides both ASAT and BMD capabilities.

In terms of space operations and total annual satellites launched to orbit, Russia in recent years falls a poor third behind the U.S. and China, with the American SpaceX firm and its ubiquitous Starlink microsat initiative comprising the vast majority. Likewise, Russia launched twenty-two successful space rocket launches in 2022, well behind the U.S. with eighty-seven and China with sixty-four, its low count partially reflecting cancelled opportunities due to the Ukraine war. SpaceX Falcon payload costs to orbit are now cheaper than those of the workhorse Proton-M and Soyuz-2, and while by 2013 nearly half of all global commercial launches were on Russian launchers, this market share is now rapidly dwindling away. In terms of innovation, Russia has been slow to implement new reusable technologies that would be cost competitive with SpaceX.

However, Russia along with the United States and China remain the only nations capable of independent human space flight. The Russian Mir scientific microgravity research space station was assembled and operated in low earth orbit from 1986 to 2001. Successor to the Salyut space station series, it was the first truly modular space station and until the development of the ISS it was the largest structure assembled in space and the first continuously inhabited with records set for long duration space flight. Cooperation with NASA Mir's assembly and with the US STS led to a further major role for Russia with the ISS.

Russia to date has provided the propulsion and maneuver capability for the ISS including reboost, attitude control, and debris avoidance through its Russian Segment, as well as fuel and other resupply through Progress tankers. The Russian Segment controls ISS navigation, guidance and control, and is comprised of six modules for operations, cargo storage (with Strela cargo cranes), docking, crew accommodations, energy and power, and scientific research activities. There were plans for additional Russian modules but these have not materialized due to the Ukraine war. Over forty cosmonauts have visited and crewed the ISS conducting various research projects on human biology, geophysics, earth resources, space biotechnology and other fields. Russia has allowed a number of paying space tourists aboard the ISS, and in 2021 hosted Russian actors for the first theatrical motion picture partially shot in space, the Russian film "The Challenge". After the end of the U.S. space shuttle STS program in 2011, Russia provided all crew and supply missions to the ISS by venerable Soyuz and Progress spacecraft until the Americans regained this capability with the SpaceX Dragon in 2020. The Roscosmos RKA Mission Control Centre in Moscow has provided active mission control for the ISS, and Star City also in Moscow remains the centre of cosmonaut skills development at its Yuri Gagarin Cosmonaut Training Centre.

Russia has indicated that it will withdraw from the ISS after 2024 leaving the space station's future in doubt. A Russian Orbital Service Station in a 400 kilometre Sun-synchronous orbit with seven modules, some originally intended for the ISS, has been planned as their alternative to the ISS by 2035. It is to be multipurpose including large spacecraft assembly, tests and launches, inter-orbital space tug operations, space science and detailed earth observations, and could even include a space tourism module. This may be developed in coordination with the International Lunar Research Station initiative agreed to by Roscosmos and the China National Space Administration in 2021, and which could have facilities in lunar orbit and on the lunar surface by the 2030s. This lunar initiative is now reportedly open to all international partners and will entail scientific activities and support, operations and cislunar transportation facilities.

The Orel crewed partially reusable spacecraft, similar in concept to the U.S. Orion capsule, is under development by Roscosmos and is intended as a replacement in different variations for both the crewed Soyuz capsule and robotic Progress cargo vehicles. Optimized for long term missions, it could be used to send cosmonauts to lunar orbit to support a proposed Lunar Orbital Station in competition with the American Lunar Gateway programme, as well as further lunar initiatives with the Chinese in competition with the U.S. Artemis initiative. The first launch of Orel could be on an Angara A5 from Vostochny Cosmodrome later this decade. A competing winged aerospacecraft shuttle design, Kliper, did not proceed beyond initial development.

The Angara and new Soyuz-2 series launch vehicles have been under steady development to replace several legacy systems. The objective of the new Angara launcher series is also to obtain an independent launch capability within Russia proper without the need for the Baikonur Cosmodrome in Kazakhstan and the Vostochny Cosmodrome is intended as its primary launch site. The Soyuz series in its differing variants remains the world's most successful launch vehicle with over 1,900 orbital flights since 1966.

The Soyuz-7 or Amur series of two stage to orbit medium lift launch vehicles is currently under development and is to be methane-oxygen fuelled and partially reusable along the lines of SpaceX's Falcon 9. A Baikal flyback reusable booster has been developed for the Angara launcher but currently lacks funding to proceed. The Angara A-5 can lift over twenty-four tons to low earth orbit and several test launches were successfully initiated since 2014 representing Russia's heaviest launch vehicle operations since the 1980s Energia. Very heavy launch vehicles are under development again and include the Soyuz-5 Super Heavy Yenisei (80 to 180 tons to low earth orbit) and Angara-100 (100 or more tons to LEO), with tests for these likely not materializing until at least 2030. Applications for such launchers could include a revived human lunar programme, interplanetary payloads, large military and civilian satellites, and space telescopes.

The Luchs Satellite Data Relay Network in geosynchronous orbit is used for various telecommunications between Russian space stations and other satellites and Earth, similar to the U.S. Tracking and Data Relay Satellite System. The advanced Luch-4 is to employ large diameter unfurlable antenna reflectors and electric propulsion systems for maneuvers and could also have military signals intelligence capabilities. The networked Centre for Deep Space Communications and it's key Yevpatoria RT-70 and Galenki RT-70 radio telescopes are leftovers from the 1970s and represents an important area that needs strengthening into something like NASA's or China's deep space communications networks with advanced ground and relay satellite systems if Russia decides to once again seriously undertake planetary research.

In recent decades Russia's scientific planetary exploration has been in relative decline. Roscosmos Director General Yury Borisov blamed the sudden failure of the Luna-25 mission in 2023, the first such Russian lunar mission since 1976, on the lack of ongoing support for lunar exploration although planning began during the 1990s. This failure could have been a result of more resources being focused on first the Mir space station and then the ISS, as well as military space to the detriment of planetary missions. The chronic misappropriation of funds that should have been used for spacecraft refinement is another possibility. Launched from the new Vostochny Cosmodrome in the far eastern Amur region, it was to be the first spacecraft to land on the unexplored lunar southern pole, but on August 19, 2023, it crashed into the lunar surface due to a failed orbital maneuver. Within days after the setback, two of the elderly space scientists close to the mission, Mikhail Marov age 90 and Vitaly Melnikov age 77, took seriously ill in quick succession and in the case of Melnikov died.

To add to Russia's humiliation, India's Chandrayaan-3 lander successfully touched down in the same polar region a few day later. The Russian failure must also be considered in the context of the 1970 Soviet Luna-16 mission that successfully returned lunar samples to Earth to grasp the full scale of lost capabilities. Russia has indicated that there will be future follow-on orbital, lander, rover and sample return lunar missions in the form of Luna-26, Luna-27 and Luna-28, with even a robotic lunar base called Luna-Glob planned for the 2030s as a prelude to crewed missions. However, planned lunar cooperation with China may now supplement, absorb or supersede these and other Russian proposed lunar initiatives.

Russia's attempt at Mars missions in 1996 and 2011 both resulted in failures with the Russian spacecraft failing to leave low earth orbit, but has had some success with several other European Mars missions launched on Russian rockets. Russia proposed an international Mars Piloted Orbital Station mission in 2005 where a large crewed spacecraft would orbit Mars for observations and employ robotic sample return landers and rovers before returning to Earth, but it did not leave the concept stage.

Various planned interplanetary missions have been cancelled due to a lack of funding and the withdrawal of international partners, including Russian participation in the pan European ExoMars 2022 mission that was suspended due to the Ukraine war. A Venera-D Venus orbiter and lander mission had been planned for 2029, but its status is unclear due to the cancellation of planned cooperation between the Space Research Institute of the Russian Academy of Sciences and NASA.

In attempting to forecast the future of the Russian space programme I will this time refrain from any grand expectations, although some disruptive surprises may still be in store. While Russian scientists and engineers are capable of great innovation, money continues to be a constraint for the realization of many grand ideas.

I do believe that as Russia's relations with the West continue to deteriorate as a result of the Ukraine war, space cooperation with financial and technology support will not come from this direction for the foreseeable future. The 2020 Artemis Accords orchestrated by the U.S. to develop a common rules based order for the exploration and development of space has not been ratified by Russia and China who feel that it is an attempt to develop international space laws that favour the Americans and their allies for activities such as lunar and asteroid mining.

With Russia's rapidly developing military alliance with near hyperpower China and Russia's key role in promoting the development of the BRICS economic bloc, Russian space ambitions will become more closely linked with those of major space player China and potentially elements of the Global South. It is also quite possible that Russia could offer nations such as North Korea and Iran assistance for their space launch and missile programmes in exchange for military assistance with the Ukraine war. Towards this end, President Vladimir Putin met with North Korean supreme leader Kim Jong Un at the showcase Vostochny Cosmodrome in September 2023 to ink a partnership deal that would see the exchange of North Korean artillery ordnance for Russian space and other advanced technologies, a move with profound strategic ramifications.

The International Lunar Research Station and related initiatives could pave the way for large scale China-Russia cooperation. With China now in a new de facto Moon race with the Americans it is not inconceivable, failing another Black Swan event, that Chinese taikonauts and Russian cosmonauts could one day explore new worlds together.

Ronald D. Humble
September 2023

THE
SOVIET
SPACE
PROGRAMME

RONALD D. HUMBLE

R
ROUTLEDGE
London and New York

First published in 1988 by
Routledge
a division of Routledge, Chapman and Hall
11 New Fetter Lane, London EC4P 4EE

Published in the USA by
Routledge
a division of Routledge, Chapman and Hall, Inc.
29 West 35th Street, New York NY 10001

Printed and bound in Great Britain by
Biddles Ltd, Guildford and King's Lynn

British Library Cataloguing in Publication Data

Humble, Ronald D.
   The Soviet space programme.
   1. Space warfare. Military policies of
Soviet Union
   I. Title
   358'.8'0947

   ISBN 0-415-02109-X

Library of Congress Cataloging-in-Publication Data

Humble, Ronald.
   The Soviet space programme / Ronald D. Humble.
      p. cm.
   Bibliography: p.
   Includes index.
   ISBN 0-415-02109-X
      1. Astronautics — Soviet Union. 2. Astronautics, Military —
Soviet Union. I. Title.
TL789.8.S65H86 1988
333.9'4'0947–dc19   88-23935
                                        CIP

   ISBN 0-415-02109-X

Contents

List of figures

Acknowledgements

Sincere thanks are extended to Reta Owens, Gord Neilson, and Henri Gibson for the invaluable assistance they provided to me in the preparation of this book.

Introduction

Why is a study of the strategy and underlying goals of the Soviet space programme important? A graphic answer lies on a Moscow avenue called Mira Prospekt where a permanent exhibition of Soviet economic achievement, a gleamng silver monument commemorating the first human orbital space flight, soars 30 metres over the city. This monument, which honours Yuri Gagarin's spectacular inaugural flight of 12 April 1961, somehow also augurs Soviet potential for executing other great space achievements. This Soviet potential, however, is largely unknown to the west. Even though future Soviet space developments may affect their future in many ways, the vast majority of citizens from the west are either ignorant or only vaguely cognizant of current and future Soviet space capabilities.

The purpose of this book then is to analyse and shed light on the current strategic nature of the Soviet space programme and to speculate on its future directions. Critical elements such as political, military, and civilian goals, force structures and organizations, technologies and doctrine are highlighted. The book also demonstrates the potentially profound impacts that such developments could have on the west.

The current use of space by the major powers for military, scientific, commercial, and political prestige purposes is steadily growing in importance. Military space strategy is turning attention not only to methods of direct intervention on Earth, but also to controlling both specific strategic defiles in space and corresponding access to and routes between key points. Comparisons can be made with the great maritime powers of history which used specific capabilities, such as fleets of warships and strategic naval bases along with merchant trade, to maintain their position of power. Traditionally international power politics emphasized the monopoly of the instruments of power by the dominant nations, and the denial to other nations of the ways and means of exercising geo-political influence. Today, the United States and the Soviet Union virtually hold monopoly positions in all aspects of manned and unmanned spaceflight, and are threatened only by gradual inroads from Europe, Japan, and China. However, unlike the United States, Soviet superpower status is based primarily upon their ability to deploy weapons of mass destruction on a global scale, rather than on additional outstanding economic, cultural, and scientific achievements that have been widely adopted by the global community. The Soviet space programme is clearly an integral component of its grand strategy for maintaining and extending its position as a great power. The Soviets have signalled their intention and ultimate capabilty to control space.

The current work examines the key elements of the grand Soviet space strategy. Given the interrelated natures of these key elements, a broad view of various Soviet space-related activities is considered. Chapter 1 provides an overall historical perspective of Soviet space strategy from its nineteenth-century roots to the early 1980s. Chapter 2 outlines Soviet scientific activity and military, civilian, and scientific organizational structures and facilities related to space activities. Soviet military doctrine and military space activities, the Strategic Rocket Forces, and ballistic missile defence (BMD) efforts are discussed in Chapter 3, 4, and 5. Chapter 6 investigates Soviet space operations, including current and future launch vehicles, manned space stations, commercial activities, and international co-operation within and outside of the Communist Bloc. With an emphasis on possible Martian exploration plans, Chapter 7 summarizes current and future scientific and interplanetary exploration. In conclusion, Chapter 8 offers an explanation of the grand strategy of the Soviet space programme, including forecasts of future military, civilian, and scientific capabilities, objectives, and technologies. Throughout the book comparisons are made between the US and other international space programmes.

A note on methodology and references is called for. Only unclassified sources of data have been used. This has been benefited by the recent Soviet trend towards increased candour and access to western journalists on the civilian and scientific aspects of their space programme. While this study has made every effort at technical accuracy and coherence, many areas, by their very secretive nature, are not subject to final determination, and not every expert observer would agree with the interpretations offered here. It is hoped that at least food for further debate will be offered.

1

Historical overview

KONSTANTIN EDVARDOVICH TSIOLKOVSKII

Much of the scientific basis for today's international space efforts was laid by three far-sighted men: the German, Hermann Oberth (1894–   ); the American, Robert Hutchings Goddard (1882–1945); and the Russian, Konstantin Edvardovich Tsiolkovskii (1857–1935). His efforts laid the foundations for today's Soviet space activities, and his influence was fully recognized in his own lifetime.

Tsiolkovskii was born to poor parents in Ijevski village of Riazon Province, Russia.[1-3] Although half deaf and lacking a formal education, he passed the required qualifying examinations and was granted a certificate for teaching high school mathematics and physics, which he did for nearly forty years in rural seclusion. However, like his father, Tsiolkovskii was a part-time inventor and a great thinker, although thought by many to be of a rather eccentric nature. Much of his early effort was devoted to the theoretical development of metal dirigibles, and he was amongst the first to conceive of using a wind tunnel for aeronautical research purposes.

In 1881 he submitted a series of papers to the St Petersburg Society for Physics and Chemistry. These papers expounded various theories of gases and new methods for measuring the velocity of light. While Tsiolkovskii's ideas were brilliant and based upon calculations thought to be original to himself, these same concepts had been discovered twenty-four years earlier in the west. Isolated from the mainstream scientific community Tsiolkovskii unknowingly reinvented these ideas.

By the 1890s, through a great leap of imagination, Tsiolkovskii proposed the exploration of space by rockets in a series of theoretical papers. In particular, 'Investigation of cosmic space by reactive machines', written in 1881 and later published in the journal

Scientific Survey (1903), 'cautiously expressed' his conjectures on the technical requirements for manned space flight. These ranged from the development of liquid-fuel rockets, staged rockets, and theoretical rocket performance parameters, to the design of sealed spaceship cabins with pure oxygen atmospheres.

Tsiolkovskii also examined such advanced concepts as satellites, the theory of geo-synchronous orbits, colonizing the solar system, and many of the practical details of living in the weightless space environment (such as taking a bath). He speculated that extraterrestrial civilizations may exist at various developmental levels:

> Is it possible that Europe is inhabited and other parts of the world are not? Is it possible for one island to be inhabited and other islands to be uninhabited? . . . All the phases of the development of life may be found on the various planets. . . . Did man exist several thousand years ago and will he be extinct in several million years? . . . . This entire process may be found on other planets.[4]

In his book *Dreams of the Earth and Sky* (1895), Tsiolkovskii predicted that eventually mankind would employ all of the energy from the Sun by colonizing the entire solar system, using asteroids and other larger planets for material to construct space cities. These ideas are remarkably similar to those popularized by the American, Dandridge M. Cole, in the 1950s and more recently Gerard K. O'Neill and Freeman J. Dyson.

While virtually ignored by the tsarist regime, Tsiolkovskii caught the imagination of and was officially popularized by the new Soviet government after 1917 and until his death. The importance of the legacy of his genius for the modern Soviet space effort is that it provides a father figure of historical legitimacy and continuity comparable to Goddard and Oberth in the west — it is the Russian destiny to explore and conquer space as outlined by this early theorist. However, it was up to others to develop the actual hardware to do so.

EARLY DEVELOPMENTS

The Latvian Friedrich Tsander was amongst a select group who had studied Tsiolkovskii's writings and led the practical work on Soviet rocket design that began in the 1920s.[5] As early as 1924 he made detailed proposals for a spacecraft, and in 1929 had developed a large model. Significant hardware development began in 1929 at

Leningrad's Gas Dynamic Laboratory in liquid propellant and electric rocket motors. The first working liquid model engine was completed by 1931, and experimental work had been completed on cryogenic oxidizers (liquid oxygen) and hypergolic (self-igniting) systems. This is the period in which the infamous 'Chief Designer' of the future Soviet space programme, Sergei Pavlovich Korolev, first became active in rocket research, as well as Valentin Glushko, who would later be active in rocket engine design.

By 1933 the first free flight of a Russian liquid fuel rocket took place near Moscow, largely a result of the enthusiasm of Soviet Armaments Minister Mikhail N. Tukhachevskiy.[6] He was interested both in rocket weapons and an early Soviet lead in space exploration. There is evidence that as a consequence of these activities the Soviet Union clamped a security cover on rocket propulsion technology as early as 1935.[7] This early interest in military applications for rockets was not unusual as Russia has a great artillery tradition, and rockets had been used in various forms as artillery for centuries. However, this research ended in 1937 as a result of the Stalinist purges of the Soviet military and the resulting imprisonment or execution of many key players. Significant Soviet research did not resume until after the end of the Second World War. During this war an emphasis was placed on the development of simple tactical weapons such as the solid fuel 'Katyusha' barrage rocket. In the mean time, the Germans had made great progress in modern rocket design. By 1945 the Soviets had formed a special team, the so-called Special Technical Commission, to locate and exploit German rocket development teams, production facilities, and technical information.

THE BEGINNING OF THE SPACE AGE

Shortly after the Second World War the Soviets began the development of a new rocket based upon their own pre-war research and captured German technology. The performance of the German V-2 had greatly impressed Joseph Stalin, as had the destructive potential of nuclear weapons. In addition, the Soviets had no reliable long-range bombers (such as the United States had developed for their Strategic Air Command) that could deliver the large and heavy nuclear weapons of the era. Therefore, mating such a nuclear weapon with a powerful rocket carrier seemed to be a natural combination that could technologically bypass the manned bomber. An intercontinental ballistic missile (ICBM) programme was evidently undertaken even

3

before the Soviets had developed effective nuclear weapons (the first Soviet atomic bomb was exploded in 1949). This was clearly an attempt at *military technological pre-emption* over the United States.

The 'NII-88' missile research organization was established at Kaliningrad in 1946, and is credited with conducting the majority of early ICBM work under the direction of the OKB-1 design bureau based in Moscow, and the overall control of L.P. Beria, head of the national security force (NKVD). Initially the ICBM programme produced a series of improved versions of the German V-2. This effort was managed by Sergei Korolev who remained a key figure in the Soviet space programme until his untimely death in 1966.[8] The original Soviet ICBM eventually produced was the SS-6 'Sapwood' (western classification; called 'Vostok' by the Soviets when displayed in Paris in 1967). On 27 August 1957 the SS-6, which employs liquid oxygen and hydrocarbon (kerosene) fuel, attained intercontinential distances, and on 4 October 1957 was used to launch Sputnik 1 into orbit. The same vehicle with an improved upper stage launched Major Yuri Gagarin into orbit. This series of launch vehicles has remained a mainstay of the Soviet space programme, with particular contemporary application as a launcher for the Soyuz manned vehicle, thus attesting to its sound initial design (and intention to deliver heavy military warheads).

Premier Nikita Khrushchev further guided the Soviet Union towards a military strategy dependent upon ICBMs. Khrushchev 'virtually rammed rockets down the throats of Red Army traditionalists'.[9] He was instrumental in the development of a new branch of the Soviet Armed Forces, the Strategic Rocket Forces, commanded first by Marshal Nedelin and later Marshal Nikolai I. Krylov. In 1962 a book appeared entitled *Military Strategy*, edited by Marshal of the Soviet Union V.D. Sokolovskii, former Chief of the Soviet General Staff and First Deputy Minister of Defence.[10] This book, in which Sokolovskii and other Soviet military leaders discuss the dramatic shifts in military thinking initiated by Khrushchev during the 1950s, has come to be regarded as a seminal official statement on Soviet military and strategic policy. This shift in military thought, in broad terms, was from the Soviet preoccupation with theatre land warfare, as exemplified during the Second World War, to global warfare involving ICBMs and nuclear warheads. Future wars would be short and decisive, with an emphasis on combined nuclear-conventional operations, first-strike blows to cripple the enemy decisively, and aggressive, unrelenting offensive actions. To this end, Khrushchev drastically reduced the size of the land army, and increased the Soviet warfighting emphasis on ICBMs and nuclear weapons. Such change was not whole-heartedly welcomed by all factions of the Soviet military. However, with its beginnings in the 1950s, the Soviet-American 'space race' accelerated during the 1960s, partially as a contest for international political prestige, and partially through true fear of each opponent's gaining military supremacy through the mastery of space technology.

The period was characterized by Khrushchev's blustering 'rocket-rattling' statements:

> The Soviet Union launched an intercontinential ballistic missile, the testing of which yielded positive results. We can now send a missile to any point on the globe, carrying, if necessary, a hydrogen warhead. Our announcement to this effect was greeted by disbelief and regarded as an attempt by Soviet leaders to instill confidence in their own people and intimidate the Western governments. But then the Soviet Union, using the intercontinential ballistic missile, launched an artificial earth satellite, and when it started circling the globe and when everyone — unless he was blind — could see it by looking up to the sky, our opponents became silent.[11]

This aggressive Soviet strategic posture stimulated similar developments in the United States, and scientists in both countries based plans for space exploration upon increasingly powerful military boosters and other dual application technologies. It has been noted that this relationship between military vehicles and exploration has had many other historical precedents such as exploratory sailing ships derived from military vessels, and the development of commercial aircraft from military aviation technology.[12] Since these beginnings the Soviet unmanned and manned space effort has received strong political support, despite various setbacks, and has produced many successes.

Appendix A provides a summary of Soviet space activities from 1957 to 1987. In general, Soviet manned and unmanned space activities are very complimentary, and often make use of dual hardware. For example, the manned Soyuz spacecraft series made use of the on-board guidance and control system that was tested by the unmanned Cosmos 186 and 188 and Cosmos 212 and 213 satellite missions that rendezvoused and docked automatically in October 1967 and April 1968 respectively. This trend continues to this day.

UNMANNED SPACE ACTIVITIES

The Soviet unmanned space programme began with Sputnik 1, which ushered in the Space Age with thirty years of important activities in science, applications (such as communications and remote sensing), and defence.[13] While Sputnik 1 was the world's first artificial satellite, it was also the first satellite used for space science to assist in the investigation of atmospheric phenomena during the International Geophysical Year (1 July 1957 to 31 December 1958). This was the beginning of the Soviet Earth orbital space science programme which subsequently involved satellites launched under the Cosmos and Intercosmos designations, the later series indicating co-operative international flights. The Cosmos and Intercosmos spacecraft are similar to the US Explorer series, generally being single-purpose satellites optimized for specific missions. In addition, the Cosmos name has historically been used as a convenient general cover for various military missions, and as a means of concealing inevitable mission failures (in particular interplanetary probes that fall off-course). Since the series began in 1962, over 700 Cosmos-designated satellites have been launched, with the non-military vehicles being used for a wide range of significant research activities. Scientific missions emphasize research on space and upper atmosphere phenomena, technical spacecraft developmental work, and space applications experiments related to Earth sciences and the Soviet national economy.

Other significant Earth orbital space science satellites include the Prognoz and Astron satellite series, which are observatory class satellites with multiple scientific objectives, such as X-ray, ultra-violet, and radio frequency astronomy. In general, the United States believes it has progressed further than the Soviets during the past three decades in unmanned Earth orbital space science, although much of the scientific activity of the Cosmos series goes unreported in the west.

Although unsuccessful in sending cosmonauts to or around the Moon, the Soviets had a very active programme of unmanned lunar probes from 1959 to 1976. Planning for this programme was probably initiated in the early 1950s. Probes included Luna 1 (January 1959), the first man-made object to reach and fly past the Moon; Luna 3 (October 1959) returned the first pictures of the far side of the Moon; and Luna 10 (March 1966), the first spacecraft to go into lunar orbit. Various Luna missions included lunar flybys, hard landings, and soft landings. Two different types of lunar landers were developed. One was for automated sample returns, in which three out of six sample missions were successfully completed in 1970, 1972, and 1976 by

6

Lunas 16, 21, and 24. A total of approximately 330 grams of lunar material was returned to Earth. The second lunar series deposited roving robotic vehicles called Lunokhods for long-term studies of the lunar surface (Lunas 17 and 21 in 1970 and 1973). No Soviet lunar flights have occurred since the last successful sample return in 1976, although, as discussed later, the Soviets are likely planning future unmanned and manned missions.

In other planetary explorations the Soviets have focused on Mars and Venus, and have not attempted to explore the inner and outer Solar System by sending spacecraft to Mercury and the outer planets. In contrast, the Americans have made significant efforts to explore the outer planets through the successful Pioneer and Voyager series of probes.

Past Soviet Martian efforts have been larely unsuccessful, compared to the successful US Mariner and Viking series. In total the Soviets officially admit to launching seven probes to Mars: one in 1962; two in 1971 (combination orbiter-landers, but without life-detection biological experiments such as carried by the two US Viking orbiter-lander probes in 1975 and 1976); and four in 1973. Only Mars 5, which provided some orbital photographs of Mars of excellent quality, is considered to be a complete success by western standards, although the Soviets claim most of their missions returned new, useful data. Two of the landers (Mars 3 and 6) made successful landings, but contact was lost shortly before or after touch-down in each case. The primary Soviet problem appears to have been targeting their spacecraft properly and ensuring the proper functioning of the braking rockets for landing. The Soviet technique was to separate the lander from the orbiter mother-ship for a direct approach to the planet before achieving orbit, whereas the United States has had consistent success with placing the entire vehicle into a parking orbit, thus providing time for fine-tuning adjustments before making a descent. For Soviet lunar exploration, this more sophisticated parking-orbit technique was successfully employed from Luna 16 onwards. Like the United States, the Soviets consistently prefer to operate planetary probes in pairs to compare the accuracy of data transmissions and increase mission success rates.

Considerable Soviet effort has been spent over the past two decades persistently studying the atmosphere and surface of Venus. While the United States has sent five probes to Venus, the Soviets have launched at least sixteen Venera spacecraft between 1961 and 1983. In general, these efforts have proven much more fruitful than their past Martian exploration. Despite early failures, Soviet scientists painstakingly

7

persisted in utilizing the knowledge gained in each mission to improve the spacecraft and techniques for subsequent missions. The images returned by Veneras 9 and 10 in 1975 were the first sent from another planet, the spacecraft having landed before the US Viking probes reached Mars. The pictures sent back were surprising because they indicated a geologically active planet with sharp rock surfaces, instead of the geologically 'dead' planet with rocks eroded by harsh climatic conditions that was expected. In addition, it was shown that the surface brightness of Venus was much greater than expected by Veneras 13 and 14 returning colour photographs of the reddish-orange surface and atmosphere, in addition to conducting soil analysis. The Soviets continued their Venusian exploration programme in 1983 with Veneras 15 and 16, which were significantly different from previous Venus probes in that both were orbiters carrying side-looking radars for mapping the surface of the planet, and in 1985 with the highly publicized Vega 1 and 2 missions to both Venus and Halley's Comet.

The Soviet Union, like the United States, has a large space applications programme which includes communications, meteorology, navigation, Earth resources, geology and mapping, and space manufacturing. The United States believes it now leads the Soviet Union in space applications. In addition, the Soviets have a very vigorous military space programme which includes reconnaissance, communications, and space weapons elements. The world's first purely military satellite was Cosmos 4, launched on 26 April 1962, which had the task of measuring radiation before and after US nuclear tests. In many respects the practical use of applications and military space systems are closely related.

MANNED SPACE ACTIVITIES

The Soviet manned space effort began with the launch of Vostok 1 on 12 April 1961 at 10:07 hours local time at the Tyuratam Cosmodrome in Kazakhstan. Cosmonaut Gagarin's single orbit lasted 108 minutes, and shocked the west because of the apparent unexpectedness of the event. While planned in secrecy the Soviets had signalled their intentions, as they did for Sputnik 1, which observers in the west had generally preferred to dismiss as propaganda. Unlike its US counterpart, the Soviet manned space programme never lost this early momentum despite several grievous setbacks.[14] These known setbacks included various docking failures, and accidents which claimed the lives of at least four cosmonauts. Only today are many

8

of the details concerning these early Soviet missions coming to light. For example, it was widely believed at the time of Gagarin's success that the Soviet Vostok launch vehicle was vastly more powerful than any available to the west in the foreseeable future. However, today it is known that the US Saturn 1 rocket first launched on 27 October 1961 was more powerful than the Vostok launcher.

While losing the so-called 'Moon Race' to the United States, the Soviets have steadily cultivated very far-reaching plans for their manned programme.

To date all Soviet manned space missions have used spacecraft consisting of expendable re-entry capsules with orbital laboratory/workshop/command modules. The main spacecraft series have been Vostok, Voskhod, and Soyuz (including the up-rated Soyuz-T and Soyuz-TM series) which are roughly comparable to the US Mercury, Gemini, and Apollo series of the 1960s and 1970s. Despite various setbacks and failures, the Soviets have perfected this system of space transportation over the past three decades, incorporating new technical systems to their basic designs as these become available.

There were six Vostok ('East') launches in all between April 1961 and June 1963, the term applying to both the spacecraft orbited and the launch vehicle. The goals of this series were similar to the US Mercury programme: to determine the basic parameters of human reactions to spaceflight through the use of automatic spacecraft (with minimal human flight input), and various astronomical and geophysical studies. Vostok 6 carried the world's first woman into space, Cosmonaut Valentina Tereshkova, on 16 June 1963. After the Vostok series came two more launches of what many analysts believe to be the same basic spacecraft, but renamed Voskhod or 'Sunrise' (no clear pictures of the vehicle have ever been released). It is widely thought that these two flights were encouraged by Khrushchev to produce new space firsts for political glorification.

These included the first multiple crew of three cosmonauts (likely without spacesuits because of the cramped space) on Voskhod 1 (12 October 1964), and the first extravehicular activity on Voskhod 2 (18 March 1965) with a spacewalk performed by Cosmonaut Alexei Leonov. While critics of Soviet manned space efforts charge that many of these flights have been motivated for non-technical reasons, similar charges can be made against US manned efforts including all the programmes from Mercury through Apollo to Space Shuttle. Such critics, many of which are advocates of unmanned space activities using robotic systems, often ignore the long-range goals underlying manned activities.

9

The Voskhod flights were the last made under the leadership of Sergei Korolev, and were followed by a period of manned flight inactivity for two years while the Americans forged ahead with their Gemini programme in preparation for the Apollo Moon exploration series. However, preparations for a continuation of advanced Soviet manned activities continued to be busily undertaken.

Perhaps one of the most contentious areas of the Soviet manned space programme is the question of whether they actually were racing the United States to the Moon. The historical evidence now suggests that in the late 1960s and early 1970s the Soviets executed a programme staged along the lines of Apollo. Many now believe the Soviets were racing the Americans 'neck-and-neck' almost until the Americans won the contest; we will probably never know for sure. Certainly official Soviet statements during the 'Moon Race' period suggested that they had every intention of winning this competition. Five Zond spacecraft (stripped-down versions of the manned Soyuz spacecraft) flights from 1968 to 1970 were identified as engineering tests related to the development of manned lunar spacecraft missions, most likely an orbital circumlunar flight that would not have actually landed a cosmonaut on the Moon's surface. Several unmanned missions, Cosmoss 379, 382, 398, and 434 from 1970 to 1971, were related to lunar propulsion system/orbiter/lander tests, with Cosmos 434 being identified as 'a test of an experimental lunar cabin'. Cosmonauts are also known to have tested other lunar-mission-related hardware such as landing simulators and specialized tools and spacesuits. The major obstacle to a successful Soviet manned lunar programme was the development of a powerful heavy launch vehicle (HLV) equivalent to the US Saturn V Apollo 'moon-rocket'. However, it is now widely recognized that the Soviets suffered a serious accident in July 1969 with their early HLV exploding on its launch pad, possibly causing extensive loss of life and damage to nearby facilities, thus effectively ending their manned lunar programme of that period. Only recently have the Soviets succeeded in their HLV development efforts, and by implication may again resume their manned lunar efforts.

After the successful Apollo 11 mission, the Soviets denied they had ever participated in the Moon Race and concentrated on their manned near-Earth orbital programme. Soviet manned flights had resumed with the tragic April 1967 mission of Soyuz 1 in which cosmonaut Col. Gladimir Komarov perished during re-entry. However, the development of the Soyuz ('union') vehicle represented a significant technological development for manned Soviet spaceflight.

10

The Soyuz design with its spherical and cylindrical shapes of orbital, command/re-entry, and propulsion/instrumentation components is a logical evolutionary development of the earlier Vostok and Voskhod series, although somewhat technologically outmoded and cramped by today's US space shuttle standards. Significant reliance is still placed on automatic controls, although more recent Soyuz models allow an increasing amount of pilot control. The stalwart Soyuz design (the last brainchild of Korolev before his death) stresses modularity, which allows individual modules to be removed, replaced, and modified with minimum redesign. It is both a manned manoeuvrable spacecraft and a miniature orbital space laboratory. Although marred by various difficulties including Komarov's death, the deaths of the Soyuz 11 crew (Cosmonauts Georgi Dobrovolsky, Vladislav Volkov, and Victor Patsayev) in June 1971 due to a decompression accident during re-entry, the booster malfunction and emergency re-entry of Soyuz 18-A in April 1975, and various aborted dockings with Salyut space stations, the Soyoz series has largely met its original long-term design objectives. These included the development of sustained manned spaceflight, orbital manoeuvring, docking, scientific-technical research in near Earth orbit (NEO), and the development and servicing of manned space stations. After each set-back the Soviets prevailed and brought the Soyuz system back on line as soon as possible.

Although denied by the Soviets, it is possible that the Soyuz design was originally intended for the manned lunar programme. The unmanned Zond spacecraft, previously discussed, were apparently a modified Soyuz design. Soyuz is capable of NEO missions at altitudes up to 1,300 km, and both manual and automatic docking and manoeuvring. An important development for Soviet Salyut space station development was the adaptation of the basic Soyuz configuration into an unmanned robotic Prognoz ('progress') transport vehicle for the delivery of both spacecraft fuel and dry cargo (the command module being replaced by an extra fuel tank section). First employed in 1978 and with over two dozen subsequent Salyut and Mir space station re-supply missions, there is no vehicle comparable to the Prognoz currently in the US spacecraft inventory.

The Soyuz series has provided a number of Soviet space firsts including the first manned space docking and space-walk crew transfer with Soyuzs 4 and 5 in January 1969 (in effect the rehearsal of a space rescue mission), the joint orbital manoeuvring of Soyuzs 6, 7, and 8 in October 1969, and a number of long-duration spaceflight missions by Soyuz crews in Salyut space stations. One such space station mission by the Soyuz 26 crew with Salyut 6 lasted 97 days from

10 December 1977 to 16 March 1978, and surpassed the previous US Skylab duration records. A Soyuz spacecraft was used for the joint US/Soviet Apollo-Soyuz Test Project in July 1975, which exemplified detente in space and was the first manned international mission involving the link-up of two foreign spacecraft.[15]

The original Soyuz series ended in May 1982 on its fortieth mission, with the improved 'T' and 'TM' series becoming the standard Soviet manned space vehicle to present. After the Soyuz 11 tragedy in 1971, all Soyuzs had carried only two cosmonauts to allow them sufficient room to wear spacesuits. The Soyuz T series now carries three spacesuited cosmonauts again and incorporates various technical improvements such as modernized avionics and flight control computers, improved fuel systems compatible with Salyut space stations, and various other incremental improvements. The T series has also suffered its share of developmental problems, such as manned spaceflight's first launch-pad fire and explosion with Soyuz T-10A on 27 September 1983, which necessitated the use of the, till then untried, ejection escape tower to save the crew. However, the Soyuz series has matured into a reliable and economical space transportation system which the Soviets are understandably proud of. This series has safely flown numerous international missions to Salyut space stations with 'guest cosmonauts' from France, Poland, Czechoslovakia, East Germany, Bulgaria, Hungary, Cuba, Vietnam, Syria, and Mongolia. The technical evolution of Soyuz continues with the very recent TM model used in conjunction with the new Mir space station.

Although Soyuz provides a limited area to conduct research, and with the addition of solar panels can remain in orbit for several days, the Soviets had a strong requirement for space station facilities to conduct long-duration orbital research. Salyut development began in the 1960s, possibly originally designed to orbit the Moon as a component of a Soviet manned lunar exploration programme. However, in NEO the Salyut space station programme has methodically brought the Soviets very close to a permanently manned presence in space.

In essence, after losing the Moon Race to the United States, the Soviets shifted their manned space programme emphasis to NEO space station activities. The development of such a space station capability is actually a logical prerequisite for future manned interplanetary exploratory efforts of long duration, as opposed to short-term spectaculars such as the US Apollo programme. Salyut 1 was launched in April 1971 but its first three inhabitants died while returning to Earth in Soyuz 11. In 1973 the launches of two space stations, Salyut

2 and Cosmos 557 (an unannounced Salyut 2 back-up) ended in failure with both craft re-entering the atmosphere only weeks after being launched. However, as in the case of other Soviet failures, support for the Salyut programme never swerved, and the system was eventually perfected after the characteristic Soviet persistent development effort. With the launch of Salyut 3 in June 1974 it appeared that variations of the space station type were to be used strictly for military missions because of its very low orbit and crew composition. Salyut 5 launched in June 1976 also appears to have been military, while Salyuts 4 and 6, launched in December 1974 and September 1977, were primarily civilian oriented. The improved Salyut 7 launched in April 1982 and the recent new generation Mir space station are dual-purpose military and commercial/scientific systems.

Suffice it to say that from 1974 to 1981 twenty-one Soviet crews occupied five space stations, developing progressively longer-term stays which culminated in several lasting over 160 days in Salyut 6. Salyut 6 had two docking ports (earlier Salyuts had only one), allowing simultaneous occupation by two Soyuz crews, with a total space station crew of up to five cosmonauts, albeit in somewhat cramped quarters. Extra-vehicular activity repairs were made, and Prognoz vehicles docked regularly on re-supply missions. Salyut 6 hosted sixteen crews, including nine guest cosmonauts from other Soviet Bloc (Intercosmos) countries over a three-year, eight-month period. Aboard the various Salyuts, cosmonauts have performed micro-gravity experiments in the manufacture of semiconductors, optical glass, new alloys, and container-less ultra-clean processing, in addition to resource remote sensing, astronomy, human, animal, and plant biological experiments, and reconnaissance and other military activities. The Soviets remain firm in their conviction, as exemplified by Mir, that the steady development of a permanent manned presence in space through space station activities is the key to their future space programme developments.

2

Space programme infrastructure

THE SOVIET SCIENTIFIC MILIEU

Aero-space technology, defined in its broadest sense, synergistically employs the scientific knowledge of almost all disciplines. For example, modern spacecraft comprise state-of-the-art metallic and composite materials, avionics and computer systems, optics, propulsion, and energy systems. Space management operations centres use the most advanced planning and management techniques. The health and performance of astronauts and cosmonauts are monitored and controlled by advanced life science techniques. Many of these cutting-edge technologies have originally been developed for military and civilian space programmes and then 'spun-off' for other applications.

Hence, the general state of a nation's science and technology development capability is a direct reflection on its potential for space programme activities. The Soviet leadership believes that Soviet pre-eminence in science and technology is the single most important factor for ultimately attaining world socialism with the defeat of the capitalist system.[1] In particular, scientific-technological advances bear first of all in the military-space field as a fundamental element of efforts to attain 'military-technical superiority' and a 'correlation of world forces' favourable to the USSR.

Since the 1917 Revolution the steady development of technical means to modernize their backward nation has produced a huge technostructure that has one-quarter of the world's scientists and half of its engineers.[2] The Soviet Union was the first nation to make a national resource commitment to a directed programme of scientific-technological progress, and has historically invested 3 per cent of its gross national product (which was approximately US $2 trillion in 1984) on research and development. The Soviet Union produces more

14

college-level graduates in science and technology than any other country, with 450,000 graduates in 1983 who majored in technical areas; in the United States, with a population 85 per cent of the Soviet Union's, such graduates were fewer than 200,000. The Soviet Union is continuing to promote scientific research as a key career field and plans to increase the number of science and scientific service personnel from some 4.8 million in 1980 to 6 million in 1990, including 1.6 million scientists. The number of national research institutes doubled from 1,500 in the early 1960s to over 3,000 in 1984, including vast complexes in 'academic cities' and some 50 specialized design bureaux responsible for developing hardware to the verge of production.

Major technical projects are assured steady, multi-year funding, unlike the situation in the west where long-range technological planning is difficult to achieve because of the natural vagaries and short-term duration of democratic governments. In particular, space and military research, development, test, and evaluation programmes are characterized by stability of funding, personnel, programmes, plans, and steady growth. The increase in the number of research institutes that conduct most Soviet research projects, and that are under the jurisdiction of the Soviet Academy of Sciences, reflects a steady expansion in their research base and a significant level of capital investment.

However, it is generally acknowledged that a relatively meagre return is derived from an enormous investment of Soviet human and financial resources, and that the overall scientific and technical performance gap with the west may be increasing rather than improving.[3] Soviet researchers and technicians simply are not as productive as their less numerous western counterparts. Since the first Nobel Prize was awarded in 1901, only 10 of the 370 science prizes have been won by Russians or Soviets, while Americans have won 137. The Soviet Union is today particularly backward in the development and application of computers and related fields.

Many Soviet problems in this area can be traced to the predominant role of the state, encouraging over-centralization in all walks of life, a reinforced aversion to risk-taking, and an emphasis on theoretical pursuits (particularly in mathematics and physics) at the expense of practical development and applications. Soviet scientific research is slow to be translated into practical innovations that are diffused to the broad economy because of systemic bureaucratic obstacles, lack of communications between production organizations and researchers, lack of incentives, and inefficient resource allocations. These problems have complex historical, cultural, and political

15

roots, but have directly resulted in a situation, which is today generally recognized by the current Soviet leadership, wherein the Soviets are being rapidly surpassed by the west in broad areas of key technologies. While the Soviets clearly remain close to the west in the theoretical grasp of many technologies, they generally remain far behind in applications.

The primary performers of Soviet research and development are research institutes, design bureaux, and production associations. Activities are vertically organized, which has historically led to programmes being conducted by highly specialized groups that often are isolated and do not communicate with each other. Soviet secrecy policies, of an almost paranoic nature, encourage this scientific isolation and lack of interdisciplinary work which is so important for modern technological innovation.

Problems also include poor capital investment and a resulting lack of equipment and instruments so severe that design bureaux and research institutes often have to make these in-house; a severe shortage of computer services and automated production systems; and a reliance on a reward system that credits meeting plans and schedules rather than innovation. All science in the Soviet Union is government sponsored, and because of the nation's command economy is expected to meet preconceived goals and plans.

Nevertheless, Soviet science has achieved major accomplishments in such areas as space technology, aircraft design, fission and fusion nuclear power, directed energy systems such as lasers and particle beams, and various military systems. It is obvious much has been achieved in these high-priority areas because of the government direction of an enormous concentration of the best resources and skilled manpower, while other areas of the economy deemed not as critical are relatively neglected. The Soviet military has right of first refusal on the best native technology and scientific resources. More than half of all Soviet scientists are likely involved in military research. Over the years, this well-defined and highly capable defence/space research and development sector has evolved as essentially separate and distinct from the less capable civil sector. As compared to their western counterparts, Soviet military planners have had a distinct advantage in marshalling, focusing, and sustaining the commitment and resources required for the development of new military systems. Advantages have included long production runs, capacity for wartime surge, a full employment policy enabling design bureaux to retain both skilled manpower and floor space, and the ability of each design bureau to undertake multiple projects. Of course, the major advantage of the

16

Soviet science and technology establishment is its sheer size — good results are bound to be produced. The Soviet Union has also been blessed with a number of brilliant scientists who have been pivotal in championing their areas of research. These have included Sergei Korolev for space technology; Igor Kurchatov for nuclear power and weapons; Lev Landau the father of Soviet physics; the great mathematicians Igor Shafarevich, Andrei Kolmogorov, and Izrail Gelfand; Eugeni Velikhov for lasers; and Gaponov Grekhov for microwave efforts.

The history of the Soviet nuclear weapons programme is a good example of what they can achieve in a concerted scientific endeavour.[4] It required the United States less than four years to produce the atomic bomb, with its industry historically advanced and unscarred by war. The corresponding Soviet effort took six years (1943–9), with a relatively backward industrial infrastructure and a country brutally ravaged by war. The Soviets were subsequently the first to build nuclear power stations and nuclear-powered icebreakers. This astonishing achievement was a product of the political determination of Joseph Stalin, hardships imposed on the general population, and a good scientific foundation in theoretical nuclear physics that had been steadily funded since the 1930s.

Historically, Soviet governments appear to have appreciated the long-term value of basic research, undoubtedly because many members of the ruling Politburo have technical backgrounds, while in comparison most politicians in the west do not (for example Leonid Breshnev was educated as a metallurgical engineer and Aleksei Kosygin as a textile engineer).

Significant efforts to improve science and technology efforts are currently underway. Recently the Soviet Union has launched a major reorganization of its research and development structure based upon a newly created association management system aimed at accelerating the pace of technological innovation, in particular for weapons systems.[5] Key research, development, and test facilities engaged with military aircraft, missile, and space systems have grown at least 30 per cent from 1974 to 1984. The Soviet Academy of Sciences and other civilian research organizations have been assigned an increasing number of defence projects, to the point where the US Defense Department estimates military research and development accounts for about half of all such activities in the Soviet Union, compared with 30 per cent in the United States.

The principal purpose of the shift to the association management system is to accelerate the pace of technical progress by reducing the lead times in implementing new technologies for application by linking and co-ordinating various design, research organization, and production facilities, thus improving traditionally poor channels of communication. The Soviets are attempting to rectify past deficiencies in the traditional straight line and staff functional structure of many scientific research organizations by adopting innovative methods of management including matrix management. Such attempts at organizational change have had mixed results, and will undoubtedly face many obstacles from individuals entrenched and secure within the existing system. However, these efforts are important because they clearly demonstrate that the Soviets realize they have a problem with their science and technology infrastructure and are attempting to do something about it. The Soviet leadership under the dynamic Mikhail Gorbachev is likely to continue efforts to improve the economy and increase the practical return from investments in science and technology.

LEVEL OF TECHNOLOGICAL DEVELOPMENT

Despite these increased efforts at productivity, Soviet military and space technology generally remains behind that of the west, with the gap in technical sophistication apparently increasing. The US Defense Department has indicated that in 1980 out of thirty deployed military system technology categories, the Soviets were rated superior in seven categories, equal to the United States in nine, and gaining on the Americans in nine.[6] Superior Soviet categories included ballistic missile defence and anti-satellite systems (which had no operational US counterparts); ICBMs were rated as equal. However, in the twenty most critical basic technology areas, the Soviets were rated as superior in none, and equal to the United States in only four areas (including directed energy, nuclear warheads, and radar sensors).

To 1986 these comparisons of Soviet and American deployed systems have remained comparable, but with a growing realization that the United States is leading in virtually every basic technology that could affect military and space capabilities over the next two decades.[7] The Soviet Union matches the United States only in aerodynamics, nuclear warheads, directed energy, optics, and power source basic technologies. Soviet gains in deployed systems are often the result of incremental technological improvements to proven designs, rather than radical applications of innovative technologies.

Micro-electronics and computer technologies, clearly areas of vital importance to modern space technology, remain areas of weakness in which the Soviets trail the west, particularly the United States. While in 1965, Soviet capabilities were ten to twelve years behind that of the Americans, by the 1980s this gap was still averaging at least three to five years.[8] In specialized areas, such as 'supercomputers' that perform billions of basic operations per second, the Soviets remain at least a decade behind the west.[9] However, there is some indication that the Soviets are developing innovative software to compensate for hardware limitations in specialized areas such as digital image processing systems[10] — a logical trend for a nation that produces many great mathematicians and chess players.

TECHNOLOGY TRANSFER EFFORTS

The Russians and Soviets have a history of attempting to graft western science and its results to their society, beginning with Peter the Great in the eighteenth century. Lenin again emphasized the transfer of foreign technology after the Russian Revolution. However, this approach condemns the recipient to being dependent upon others and lagging behind in the most innovative 'leading edge' technologies.

Currently the Soviets have made vigorous, and apparently largely successful, efforts to supplement their indigenous technological capabilities with technologies acquired from the west by legal and illegal means. Legal means include various avenues of technology transfer: the direct purchase of unrestricted equipment; bilateral science and technology exchanges; student and inter-academy exchanges; attending conferences and symposia; acquiring unclassified government technical reports; and scanning the vast, and often surprisingly detailed, western professional open literature.[11] While the majority of Soviet acquisitions of western technologies are through legal means, efforts are also made to acquire directly predominately military-oriented western hardware and documents in programmes orchestrated by the Military Industrial Commission (VPK) of the Presidium of the Council of Ministers and the Ministry of Foreign Trade, and operated by the two intelligence services, the Committee for State Security (KGB) and the Chief Intelligence Directorate of the General Staff (GRU).[12]

To a degree the GRU and KGB are internally competitive organizations. The GRU is responsible for military intelligence collection and analysis, and has a staff of over 5,000 at its operational headquarters at Khodinka airfield, Moscow. The GRU is divided into over a dozen geographic and functional directorates, including the Sixth Directorate which controls military signal intelligence operations; the Ninth Directorate, which collects and analyses foreign military technologies; and the Space Intelligence Directorate. This last directorate apparently manages the Soviet space intelligence programme, including arms-verification monitoring and the research and development of new photo-reconnaissance systems. The GRU is also very active in human intelligence collection — the Second Directorate co-ordinates spying in North America.

The KGB has been described as the 'sword and shield' of the Soviet Communist Party, and has varying responsibilities such as foreign intelligence and covert actions, and internal security including the suppression of dissident movements. The KGB is estimated to have over half a million members, controlled from KGB headquarters at Dzerzhinsky Square in Moscow. Like the GRU, it is divided into geographic and functional directorates, such as the First Chief Directorate which is responsible for human intelligence and the acquisition of western defence technologies (literature, hardware, and documentation). The Eighth Chief Directorate is responsible for signal intelligence collection and analysis.

Specific western firms and universities are apparently targeted as sources of strategic technologies, in particular micro-electronics, computers, C^3I (command, control, communications, and intelligence systems), computer-integrated design and manufacturing, and materials fabrication. Soviet technical areas believed to benefit directly from acquired western technology include, in order of precedence, electronics (including integrated avionics and advanced displays), electro-optics, aviation, missiles and space systems, communications, radars and computers, and the nuclear industry and lasers.[13] It is rather unclear how successful the Soviets are at actually 'reverse-engineering' such technologies without a corresponding support infrastructure. It should be also noted that there are various western applications of transferred Soviet technologies, such as the Tokamak nuclear fusing reactor design, and directed energy weapon system components.

RESOURCE ALLOCATION

The exact funding and growth rates of Soviet scientific military and space efforts have been areas of much speculation. The US Defense Department contends that to support the continuing growth and modernization of the Soviet armed forces, the Soviet Union over the past quarter of a century has devoted an average of at least 12–14 per cent of its GNP, with a growth rate of about 3–6 per cent per year to its military, almost double that of the United States.[14] Soviet investment in general military research and development is also claimed to be twice that of the United States, with the dollar cost for the 1973–82 period totalling about $315 billion for the Soviets, compared with $185 billion for the Americans.[15] Such expenditures have been increasing in real terms of about 7 per cent for the past two decades, thereby doubling every ten years and growing more than any other Soviet military investment.[16]

Specifically in terms of the Soviet space programme, US intelligence estimates indicate that space expenditures rose from about 2 per cent of total military expenditures in 1960 to over 11 per cent in 1974, leading to an estimate of between 1 and 2 per cent of the current Soviet GNP being devoted to the space programme.[17] In real terms (US dollars) this amounts to $7 to $14 billion in 1974, $14 to $28 billion in 1980, and currently some $18 to $36 billion.[18] Such limited official Soviet space programme budget information as is available tends to support this upward trend for space programme expenditures. It can be estimated that the space programme budget is growing at a rate of over 15 per cent per year, exceeding the significant growth rate of the overall defence budget. If closely related areas such as ICBM and BMD defence activities are included, this figure would be considerably higher.

These expenditure estimates would appear to indicate that, in real terms, the Soviets are devoting much more of their economic wealth to space than the Americans who have a much larger GNP (US civilian and military space expenditures were about $15 billion during the 1983 financial year). However, such estimates for Soviet military and space monetary expenditures must be considered with some scepticism as indicators of actual effort. Analysts often take the apparent results of Soviet efforts and price them in terms of what it would cost to develop or field a western equivalent. Western and Soviet costs of production and labour are actually not directly comparable, and in particular monetary expenditures are not a valid yardstick of measurement. Perhaps the best measurements of Soviet capabilities are the actual physical size of forces in being and those being deployed and developed, technical hardware, and related research, development, and production capabilities. In terms of space technology, while the overall Soviet technical level is behind the west, they are clearly willing to do much more with what they have, and a priority on space and military research and development will likely continue unabated.

21

SPACE PROGRAMME ORGANIZATION

The government of the Soviet Union is an interrelated organization of the Communist Party, the Supreme Soviet, and the Council of Ministers. Ultimate power resides within the Communist Party, with the office of General Secretary being the pinnacle of this power. The Central Committee of the Communist Party represents the political elite of the Soviet Union. The Central Committee appoints the Politburu (political bureau), which determines national policy and priorities. The Supreme Soviet, or national legislature, is the principal organ of state. With the approval of the Politburo, members of the Council of Ministers, which administer national policy, are appointed by the Supreme Soviet. The Council elects a chairman who is the Soviet Union's chief executive officer. Within the Council are sixty-two ministries, several of which are directly involved with the space programme. Ultimate control of the Soviet space effort is to be found within this government structure.

The Soviet space programme is known to be a very large undertaking, employing hundreds of thousands of people directly or indirectly. Such a massive undertaking would appear to require a highly co-ordinated administrative and organizational structure. Although many organizations and various jurisdictions are involved, it appears multiple responsibilities are assigned to key politically acceptable individuals who have singular responsibility for the achievement of programme objectives. Certainly the Communist Party must closely control and monitor all aspects of the programme from the policy level, through research, to the shop-floor level. It has long been assumed that there is no single agency responsible for the civilian aspects of the Soviet space programme comparable to the United State's NASA, although there are current indications of change in this direction.

Both the western and Soviet public literature provides little definitive information on the administration, structure, and organization of the Soviet space programme, although there is learned speculation from several sources.[19] Figure 1 attempts to illustrate likely organizational relationships. The top decision-maker on space policy is the General Secretary, who, beginning with Nikita Khrushchev, appears to have provided strong personal support for Soviet space efforts over the past several decades. Directional responsibility for the programme lies with the entire Politburo, although the Politburo member most directly involved is likely to be the Defence Minister. The total space programme structure may even be an integral part of the Ministry of Defence. Certainly the Soviet leadership recognizes the military and technological benefits accruing from the space programme, as well as its domestic political utility and international source of prestige and goodwill.

Figure 1 Soviet space programme organization

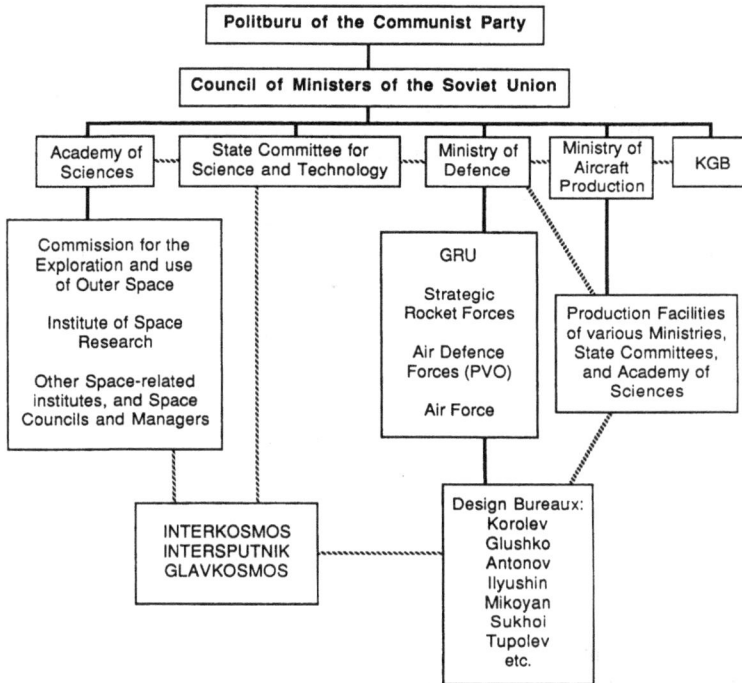

| Politburo of the Communist Party |
| Council of Ministers of the Soviet Union |

| Academy of Sciences | State Committee for Science and Technology | Ministry of Defence | Ministry of Aircraft Production | KGB |

Commission for the Exploration and use of Outer Space

Institute of Space Research

Other Space-related institutes, and Space Councils and Managers

GRU

Strategic Rocket Forces

Air Defence Forces (PVO)

Air Force

Production Facilities of various Ministries, State Committees, and Academy of Sciences

INTERKOSMOS INTERSPUTNIK GLAVKOSMOS

Design Bureaux:
Korolev
Glushko
Antonov
Ilyushin
Mikoyan
Sukhoi
Tupolev
etc.

The Council of Ministers and various state committees control many of the important research and development and operational elements of the space programme including the Ministry of Defence, the Ministry of Defence Industries, the State Committee on Science and Technology, the State Committee on Planning, the Military-Industrial Commission, the Ministry of Instrument-Making, Automation Equipment, and

23

Control Systems, and the Soviet Academy of Sciences. The State Planning Committee (GOSPLAN) is responsible for exercising budget control and planning scientific, technological and economic activities that involve numerous organizations and sectors of the economy. It is generally assumed that the space programme utilizes long-range planning and, as such, integration of it with other national undertakings could involve considerable involvement by the GOSPLAN.

The State Committee on Science and technology is the dominant co-ordinating body for primarily civilian scientific work. The committee is responsible for co-ordinating civilian research and development, establishing priorities, and introducing new technologies into industrial areas. It is probably significantly influenced by the defence establishment. While it is generally believed to have a significant space programme role, there are differing opinions on the exact nature of this involvement. Possible roles include a primary co-ordinating function; an intermediary between the programme and the government and party leadership; or merely co-ordinating some of the research and development activities associated with the space programme. Boris Tolstykh, an engineer, was appointed chairman of the committee early in 1987. He also received the position of deputy prime minister, a reflection of the committee's importance. He succeeds Gury Marchuk who headed the committee since January 1980 and was named the new President of the Soviet Academy of Sciences in October 1986.

As related in Chapter 1, there has been a very close historical relationship between the Soviet space programme and the military establishment. While the Soviets themselves claim their space efforts to be completely scientific and peaceful in nature, the military has a deep, likely dominant, relationship with the programme, although possibly sharing some organizational control with the Academy of Sciences. Military influence is directed both from the Defence Ministry and through heavy representation on steering committees for various other organizations such as the strategic hardward manufacturing industries. Many key individuals identified with the space programme have strong military or defence industry backgrounds. Until recently, it was believed the Strategic Rocket Force (a separate branch of the Soviet Armed Forces — see Chapter 4) conducted all civilian and military space launches, in addition to spacecraft tracking and launch facility duties. The Soviet Air Force is responsible for cosmonaut training at Zvezdnii Gorodak (Star City) near Moscow, and for recovering Earth-bound spacecraft.

The Soviet Academy of Sciences is the organization most visibly involved with the space programme, and subsidiary organizations within it are promoted by the Soviets as the equivalent of the US NASA. It is considered to be the foremost centre of fundamental and applied Soviet research and development, and consists of fourteen Republic academies and seven branches. The Academy provides a co-ordinating function for the pure scientific research activities of its various associated organizations, which in all incorporate 250 scientific institutions employing over 160,000 staff, 40,000 of which are professional researchers. While there is no doubt of its extensive space programme involvement, through research and development, consultation and international public relations, its central organizational role is questionable. However, within the Academy are found various commissions, institutes, and organizations very directly involved with the space programme. These entities have a scientific, military, and political membership and include the Interdepartmental Commission for the Co-ordination and Control of Scientific-Theoretical Work in the Field of Organization and Accomplishment of Interplanetary Communications of the Astronomical Council of the USSR; Commission on the Exploration and Utilization of Space or Commission for the Study and Use of Outer Space (perhaps superseding the Interdepartmental Commission); Commission for the Promotion of Interplanetary Flights or Commission for Space Travel; Vernadsky Institute of Geochemistry and Analytical Chemistry currently directed by Valery Barsukov; and the Institute of Space Research currently directed by Roald Z. Sagdeev.

An important space agency within the Academy is the Council for International Co-operation in the Studies and Uses of Outer Space (Interkosmos), which is the co-ordinating body for co-operative space projects within the Warsaw Pact and satellite nations (and occasional western participation, in particular with France), which has major political significance for the Soviets. Its current chairman is V.A. Kotelnikov. Apparently related to this is the Intersputnik International Organization which is responsible for providing an international system of space telecommunications, through space satellites and ground complexes, for Communist nations and other interested parties. (The Soviet Union is also one of the largest participants in the London-based International Maritime Satellite Organization, or Inmarsat.)

A very recent Soviet space organization, apparently resulting from a broadening of the Interkosmos/Intersputnik international co-operation theme, is the Main Administration for the Creation and Use of Space Technology for the National Economy and Scientific Research (Glavkosmos).[20] Revealed late in 1985, the Soviets have stated their intention that Glavkosmos is to be their specific counter-part to NASA and other central civilian national space agencies, and will have the primary goal of managing space science and co-operative international space ventures. Its current chairman is Alexander I. Dunaev. Stated areas of responsibility include the general benefit of space technology to the Soviet economy through commercially oriented activities such as long-distance communications (including the long-distance facsimile transmission of newspapers), meteorology, land resources surveys, navigation, and the international 'Kosmos-Sarsat' satellite air-sea rescue system, in addition to the space-based production of super-pure and biologically active materials. It is offered as having a broad co-ordinative and administrative function of linking and providing a focal point for the space-related activities of various government departments and scientific institutes. Obviously military activities are ostensibly excluded. Its international scientific and com-mercial co-operative activities are to be varied in scope, such as the recent Vega Venus-Halley probes, and not restricted to Communist countries.

Glavkosmos's exact responsibility for the Soviet manned pro-gramme is unclear, however; one of its first formal actions was the signing of an agreement in March 1986 with France's CNES national space agency for the long-duration flight of a French astronaut on the new Soviet Mir space station in 1988. It will be involved with the development of manned and unmanned spacecraft and launch vehicles, the preparation for launches and the operational use of space technology. This could mean that the Strategic Rocket Forces will now launch only military missions. Glavkosmos will be complemen-tary to Interkosmos which will be responsible for actual scientific experimentation, while all related hardware will be produced under the responsibility of Glavkosmos.

Glavkosmos may also act as a facilitative contact between the Soviet industries which produce space hardware and the scientfic and other end-users — a role related to the new Soviet association management system discussed earlier. One of Glavkosmos's key stated tasks is to make contacts between Soviet industry and foreign countries in the framework of co-operative programmes, rather than having this done at the traditional ministry level. The marketing of the Proton booster as an international satellite launch vehicle (see Chapter 6), as well as soliciting international partners for a series of future unmanned scientific planetary probes are very likely activities. This is part of an apparent recent Soviet trend towards international openness, frankness, and friendliness in space science.[21] Such international

26

co-operation is beneficial to the Soviets for several reasons including cost sharing of expensive scientific pay-loads and the transfer of advanced technologies from other countries.

It is not clear whether Glavkosmos, with its focused tasks, is in actuality the central co-ordinating mechanism for the Soviet space programme in its entirety. This authoritative body would likely include high-ranking members of the Communist Party, the military, the scientific establishment, and the various sectors of the economy involved with the space programme, and would likely be directly influenced by the Council of Ministers. It would plan and control both civilian and military space activities, many of which are highly interrelated. It is not clear whether this body is formal or more *ad hoc* in nature.

Little is known to the west about the actual production of Soviet space hardware, and related organizations, but this capability is likely closely related to Soviet aircraft experimental design bureaux and production facilities.[22] Most of these facilities are located in or near Moscow, and each bureau is headed by a chief designer. It is currently estimated that as many as nine aerospace and heavy machinery design bureaux are involved with the Soviet space build-up. In many areas, Soviet aircraft manufacturing technology is equal to that of western aircraft manufacturers, with plant modernization paralleling industry growth. Current emphasis is on increased automation in production operations to improve worker productivity and plant efficiency. As discussed earlier, foreign technology is obtained when necessary to fill domestic technical gaps. The Soviet policy of meeting planned production goals and quotas has generally overshadowed quality control and assurance. However, it is known that zero-defects programmes are being established in several aircraft plants, and the Soviets are implementing industry-wide quality control standards. This has important implications for Soviet space technology production because of the emphasis placed on the assembly-line production of many launchers and spacecrafts to meet the high launch rates characteristic of the Soviet space programme.

SPACE FACILITIES

Figure 2 illustrates the geographic location of major space-related facilities in the Soviet Union. Relatively little is known of these facilities in the west. The three major launch sites are Tyuratam (Baikonur), Kapustin Yar, and Plesetsk.[23] By 1983, successful Soviet

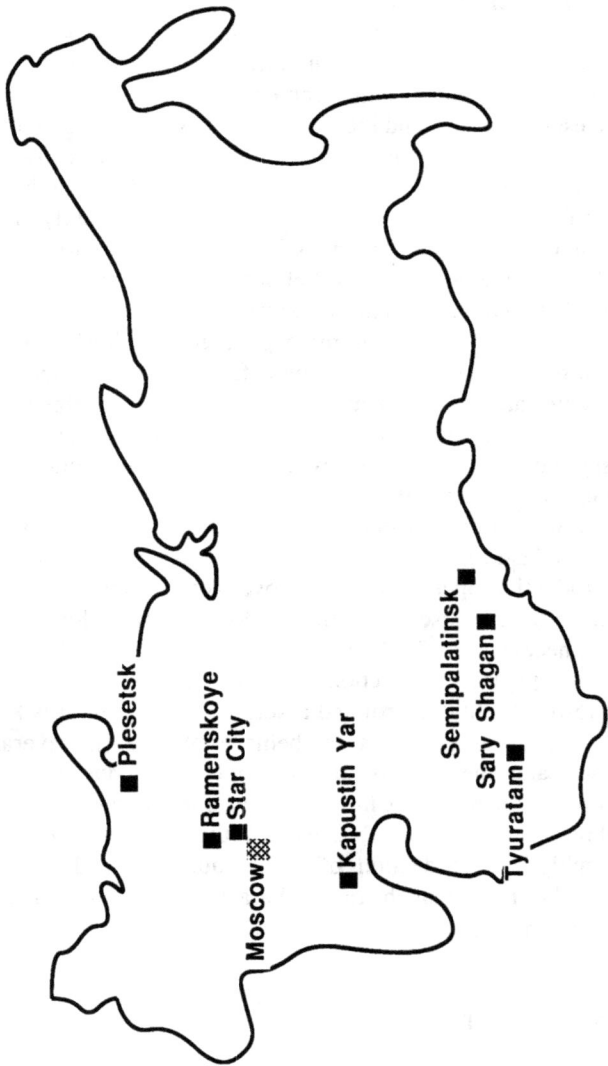

Figure 2 Soviet space-related facilities

Plesetsk

Ramenskoye
Star City

Moscow

Kapustin Yar

Semipalatinsk

Sary Shagan

Tyuratam

space launches included 626 from Tyuratam, 79 from Kapustin Yar, and 931 from Plesetsk, compared with 452 from Vandenberg Air Force Base and 344 from Cape Canaveral in the United States. Each of these Soviet complexes is protected by air-defence and surface-to-air missile systems. It is also interesting to note that each site is located at latitudes of 45 degrees or greater, thus avoiding direct launches through the radioactive Van Allen Belt, which possibly could be augmented in lethality by direct attack during a nuclear war. In contrast, the major US launch sites are well underneath this magnetospheric phenomenon.

Tyuratam is the largest and most versatile of Soviet launch sites and is the equivalent of the American Cape Canaveral. It is located near the rail village of the same name in Kazakhstan at about 45.6 N latitude, 63.4 E longitude, about 160 km east of the Aral Sea. The new town of Leninsk has been built outside the launch site to support the facility and has some 50,000 inhabitants. The Soviets refer to the site as the Baikonur Cosmodrome, although Baikonur is some 250 km to the north-east of Tyuratam, in an apparent misinformation legacy that dates from the early days of the 'space race'.[24] Tyuratam is the site from which both Sputnik 1 and Vostok 1 were launched, as were the first Soviet ICBMs, all of the early Sputniks, all subsequent manned and unmanned planetary and lunar flights, all Proton 'D' vehicle flights, and all military FOBs and ASAT tests. The facility is massive, with a maze of over 80 launch pads spread out over at least 150 by 90 kilometres. Publicly released satellite photographic imagery produced from 1983 to 1986 by NASA's Landsat 3 satellite and space shuttle Mission 9/Spacelab 1, and most recently the French Spot remote-sensing spacecraft, have confirmed past speculation that Tyuratam is the site of increased development activity for the Soviet space shuttle and large Saturn-5-class booster projects.[25] Facilities include a new 4,600 metre runway (comparable in size to NASA's Kennedy Space Center space shuttle recovery runway) for Soviet space shuttle and space-plane recovery; new launch pads for the shuttles and Saturn-5-class HLV; and a large hundred-metre-long assembly building facility comparable in size to the Vehicle Assembly Building at the Kennedy Space Center.

The Northern Cosmodrome at Plesetsk is the most important Soviet military launch site, similar in function to the US Vandenberg Air Force Base, and is the busiest space launch site in the world.[26] By 1982 over 800 pay-loads had been launched from the site. Typically over two-thirds of Soviet pay-loads are launched from Plesetsk in a given year, most of which are military in nature. It is located in

European Russia near the town of the same name on the Moscow-Archangel railway at about 62.8 N latitude and 40.1 E longitude, about 1,000 km north of Moscow. It is an operational launch site, compared to the specialized and experimental nature of many of Tyuratam's launches, and its northerly position permits communications, weather, navigation, and reconnaissance and other military satellites to be placed in polar and highly elliptical orbits. The facility is about 100 km long with at least four launch sites heavily defended by SAM batteries. Plesetsk is also believed to be an ICBM test site.

Kapustin Yar is located in European Russia on the Volga River below the city of Volgograd at about 48.4 N latitude and 45.8 E longitude. It was the first Soviet rocket development centre and was used for testing captured German V-2 rockets and various sounding rocket experiments after the Second World War. It is similar to the US Wallops Island facility. Launch activities have concentrated on small scientific Cosmos satellites, but the use of this facility has recently steadily decreased. However, Kapustin Yar is used to fire simulated ICBM attacks towards the Sary Shagan ABM test station 2,000 km to the east for test interceptions, and was the launch site in June 1982, for an unmanned sub-scale Soviet space shuttle test vehicle and subsequent related tests.

Zvezdnii Gorodak, translated variously as 'Starry Town' or 'Star City', is the Soviet Union's Manned Spaceflight Control Centre, and is located at the city of Kalinigrad some 30 km north-east of Moscow.[27] The facility is under military control, with cosmonaut General G. Beregovoy being its most recent commander and cosmonaut Valery Ryumin the flight director. It is a self-contained town employing some 2,000 people. Cosmonaut training facilities include Soyuz, Prognoz, Salyut, and Mir simulators, and a large neutral buoyancy tank containing a space station mock-up for weightlessness training. An approximate complement of fifty cosmonauts, including foreign Intercosmos and French candidates, undertake a rigorous training regime that westerners have observed stresses a repetitive learning process philosophy. The mission control centre itself is said to resemble closely a smaller version of the US Johnson Space Center in Houston (undoubtedly a spin-off from the 1975 Apollo-Soyuz Test Project), and is responsible for controlling all manned spacecraft and space station activity.

As a result of lacking the land-based global tracking and communications facilities of the United States, and because Soviet spacecraft are within direct visibility of their territory for only one out of every twenty-four hours, they have compensated for this shortcoming by constructing a fleet of over thirty space and missile monitoring and control ships. Operating under the flag of the Soviet Academy of Sciences, the flagship is the 45,000 tonne *Kosmonaut Yuri Gagarin*, which is said to have seventy-five computer-controlled aerials and eighty-six laboratories.

The Soviets also have large radar installations, the equivalent of the US BMEWS and Pave Paws systems, at Pechora near the Arctic Circle to detect ICBM attacks from the north; at Kiev to monitor the Mediterranean and the East Atlantic; and at Komsomolsk-na-Amure, north-east of the Japanese Hokkaido Island, to cover the south and south-east for SLBM attack. In accordance with the 1972 ABM treaty-ratified by the United States and Soviet Union, these facilities are on the periphery of Soviet territory and scanning outwards. However, in 1983, the United States protested that a new radar system near Abalakova in Central Siberia could be part of an ABM system for protecting a nearby SS-18 ICBM field. All of these facilities are likely-to have a space-monitoring capability.

Located in the southern Soviet Union, Semipalatinsk and Sary Shagan are highly secretive military test centres associated with nuclear weapons, BMD, ICBM, and directed-energy beam weapons research and development. Sary Shagan is situated on Lake Balkhash in Central Asia near the Chinese border and has been a test-range for anti-missile weapons for a quarter of a century. Semipalatinsk has been the site of various nuclear weapon, laser and particle-beam tests.

3

Military space

SOVIET STRATEGIC ENVIRONMENT

The Soviet strategic environment and military force structure is the
end product of various interrelated factors that have occurred during
over 1,000 years of repeated brutal historical experiences, and related
geographical, political, and cultural factors.[1] Geographically, Russia
and later the Soviet Union have occupied a centralized 'heartland'
pivotal position that lends itself potentially both to dominating the
peripheral Eurasian landmass and invasion from surrounding enemies.
The impact of the Mongol invasion and occupation of Russia in the
thirteenth century was fundamental in shaping subsequent Russian
political structures because of its imposition of a non-European
political style. While western Europe was experiencing the
Renaissance and the Reformation and the emergence of democratic
ideals, Russia was under the heel of an Asiatic military autocracy.
After the overthrow of the 200-year-old Mongol domination,
Muscovite Russia proceeded in turn to dominate neighbouring states
(for example Georgians, Armenians, and nations in Central Asia and
in the Baltic Area). Through the Russian Orthodox Church, Moscow
was characterized as the 'Third Rome'. The Tsars fostered a tradition of militarism and strict autocratic government which was encouraged by foreign invasions such as that of Napoleon's Grand Army
in 1812. History taught the Russians a clear lesson: their survival
depended upon the acquisition and use of military power. In the twen-
tieth century this Russian tradition of militarism, autocratic government, and fear of foreign invasion has been strengthened by the tragic
results of the two World Wars and the Bolshevik Revolution. The
Soviet Union of today is in many respects an imperial power with
an overlay of Communist ideology with global pretensions. The

technically advanced west, and in particular the United States, is its main current uncontrolled adversary. The Soviets recognize that Eastern Europe must be held at any cost as a buffer zone against potential enemies from the west. In this regard, there is an underlying Soviet fear of the re-emergence of a re-unified Germany as a world power. China is perceived as a secondary threat, technologically inferior, but with a serious security potential if militarily and technologically bolstered by the United States and Japan.

Colin S. Gray has outlined the fundamental characteristics of the Soviet geo-political quarrel with the west.[2] In summary, the key Soviet security characteristics are:

1 An insatiable quest for total national security that has no boundaries compatible with the security of others; hegemony is synonymous with security.

2 An assumption that international politics is a permanent struggle for power, and that war and peace and 'war in peace' (cold war) are but different phases of a continuous struggle.

3 A belief that the Soviet Union can never be militarily too strong, and that this military strength is not a threat to world peace or a source of international instability, unlike the military power of the west.

4 A strategic and political view of military strength rather than a technical view, common to the west, of what is and what is not stabilizing.

5 A confidence in unilateral military strength combined with a great unwillingness to abandon important military functions on the assumption of restraint on the part of others.

6 A constant recognition that war is always possible and that the sole duty of soldiers is to fight and win wars, given the political decision to do so.

7 A basic assumption not to design its military forces to favour criteria related to arms control and crisis management, as many propose the United States has done, but with a concern for war-waging effectiveness and military efficiency.

In summary, Soviet military doctrine and strategy is the product of the Soviet military establishment, and once the political decision to fight is made, the Soviet military is unlikely to wage war in a tentative 'limited' or 'bargaining' manner, unlike the manner proposed by current western theoretical nuclear doctrine.

SOVIET MILITARY STRATEGY

A thorough analysis of Soviet strategic thought reveals a thoughtful blend of Sun Tzu, Machiavelli, and von Clausewitz with Lenin that is directly reflected in Soviet military theory and practice. However, the basic tenets for Soviet strategy in the nuclear age were outlined in Sokolovskii's *Soviet Military Strategy* in 1962. The predominant role of nuclear weapons in modern warfare, for military operations of all types, was repeatedly stressed:

> In modern warfare nuclear weapons can be employed for various missions: strategic, operational and tactical. . . . [Nuclear weapons] permit the execution of military missions in a considerably shorter time than was possible in past wars.[3]

Together with nuclear weapons, missiles, specifically ICBMs under the control of the technologically elite Strategic Rocket Forces, are emphasized as the primary means of combat. This emphasis is often at the expense of the traditional arms of the military. For example:

> From the point of view of weapons, a third world war will be a *missile and nuclear war*. The massive use of nuclear weapons, particularly thermonuclear, will make war unprecedentedly destructive and devastating. Entire states will be wiped off the face of the earth. Missiles carrying nuclear warheads will be the main instruments for attaining the war's aims.[4]

However, it is denied that through its totally destructive nature nuclear warfare has lost its Clausewitzian significance as an instrument for political ends:

> It is quite evident that such [Western] views are the consequence of a metaphysical and anti-scientific approach to a social phenomenon such as war and are the result of the idealization of the new weapons. It is well known that the essential nature of war as a continuation of politics does not change with changing technology and armament.[5]

Soviet military doctrine is described in *Soviet Military Strategy* as being highly offensive in character to bring about the rapid defeat of the enemy. Defensive actions are taken only in support of offensive efforts, with attack being the decisive operation. Objectives are achieved through initial surprise strikes:

34

in order to annihilate the opponent or force him to surrender in
the shortest possible time . . . the annihilation of the opponent's
armed forces, the destruction of targets deep in his territory, and
the disorganization of the country will be a single, continuous process of the war. The two chief reasons are, first, the need to defeat
the aggressor as thoroughly and as quickly as possible, which
requires that he be deprived of the military, political and economic
capacity to wage war; and, second, the use of military instruments
[now] at hand might well accomplish these [military, political, and
economic] aims simultaneously.[6]

However, it has been observed that since the mid-1970s Marshal
Nikolai Ogarkov has led a school of military thought in a major
reassessment of Soviet military doctrine.[7] Doubts have been expressed on the overall utility of nuclear weapons, and arguments put forth
for solely conventional operations, at least in the initial stages of a
protracted war. In 1982 Marshal Ogarkov edited a revealing paper
entitled 'Always in Readiness to Defend the Fatherland' which outlined
the basic tenets of the new doctrine:

1 Technology is the foremost influence in military affairs, and
   military doctrine is now being driven by (non-nuclear)
   technology.
2 The current strategic situation of 'mutual assured destruction'
   (MAD) renders both the Soviet Union and the United States
   vulnerable to unacceptable damage.
3 The Soviet Union must avoid the outbreak of a nuclear exchange
   during a major conflict through decisive conventional operations, but failing this a full pre-emptive nuclear strike must be
   delivered against every nuclear force (no policy of graduated
   nuclear response, in common with *Military Strategy*).
4 The Soviet Union must be organized and prepared to fight a
   protracted war.

However, some western observers maintain that there has not actually
been a substantive deviation in Soviet strategy from the offensive
nuclear doctrine outlined by Sokolovskii.[8] Former high-ranking
Soviet GRU officer Victor Suvorov is adamant on the highly offensive, nuclear-oriented and integrated nature of current Soviet
strategy.[9] Perhaps significantly, Ogarkov was suddenly replaced as
Chief of the General Staff in September 1984.

SOVIET TECHNOLOGICAL STRATEGY

Soviet military strategy from Sokolovskii to Ogarkov has consistently reflected the importance of applying the results of scientific-technological progress towards practical military applications. *Soviet Military Strategy* states:

Mankind is entering a period of the greatest scientific and technological revolution, resulting from mastery of nuclear energy and the conquest of space, the development of chemistry, automation of industry, electronic equipment, and other notable achievements in science and technology. These developments will largely determine the nature of a future world war. . . . For this reason, military strategy cannot fail to take into account the status and prospects of the development of science and technology when investigating the possible nature of modern warfare.[10]

S.T. Possony and J.E. Pournelle enumerated in 1970 four overall aspects to military technological strategy:[11]

1 Superior forces in being.
2 Modernization of weapons.
3 Modernization of the technological base.
4 Operational capability to employ new technology.

Technological warfare was defined 'as the direct and purposeful application of the national technological base and of specific advances generated by that base to attain strategic and tactical objectives'.[12]

Possony and Pournelle describe the Soviet technological strategy as one of focusing effort on the development of specific technological achievements, working on each problem until it is solved and concentrating on a carefully chosen centre of gravity (that is Soviet space programme).[13] Simplicity of design, low costs of production and operational reliability of military technology are also important aspects of the strategy. Despite the current overall western technological lead over the Soviet Union, the Soviet technological strategy has resulted in local parity or even superiority in various aspects of military technology.

In a more recent analysis it is outlined how the Soviets compensate for technological inferiority through superiority of numbers, mass, and a synergism achieved by employing combinations of technically inferior weapons in elaborate strategic schemes to offset or overcome

36

western technological superiority in specific weapons systems.[14] The typical Soviet response to a given type of superior western military hardware is rarely an attempt to compete directly for the development of superior systems of the same type. Rather, Soviet systemic military advantages and western weaknesses are exploited, and the arms control negotiating process is used to constrain the west from the full realization of areas of apparent technological advantage (for example the Strategic Defence Initiative).

Physicist and nuclear weapons expert Freeman Dyson cautions that the Soviets also have a long tradition of promoting apparent technological advances or breakthroughs for a 'defence by bluff, the exploitation of advanced weapons of dubious military value for political and psychological reasons'.[15] The Soviets exploit new weapons developments for impressive shows of strength, even though the weapons may be prototypes and not in mass production. The total security environment in the Soviet Union often makes such mis-and-disinformation tactics very effective.

SOVIET MILITARY SPACE STRATEGY

To this day the Soviets publicly maintain that their space programme is completely peaceful in nature. However, they have long recognized the military importance of space, usually describing this awareness in terms of admonishing a potential US threat from this environment. For example *Soviet Military Strategy* states:

> Soviet military strategy acknowledges the need to study the use of space and space vehicles to reinforce the defence of the socialist countries. . . . It would be a mistake to allow the imperialist camp to gain any superiority in this area. The imperialists must be opposed with more effective weapons and methods of using space for defence. Only in this way can they be forced to refrain from the use of space for a destructive, devastating war.[16]

Western theorists have long speculated on the wide-ranging military potential of space in considerably more detail.[17] During and after the Second World War, the German aero-space engineer Eugen Sanger envisaged the development of manned antipodal rocket bombers and a variety of other military space systems, while in the 1950s the V-2 pioneer Wernher von Braun advocated the construction of manned US space stations armed with nuclear weapons. Space futurists such as Dandridge M. Cole and Michael Golovine predicted the militarization of strategic areas of space within the Earth-Moon system — the 'Panama Theory of Space'. Today, the military use of space is still at a relatively early stage of development but, as predicted by these visionaries, is steadily increasing with the passage of time.

The space environment of the Earth-Moon system can be seen as a series of *gravity well zones* that are tactically analogous to terrestrial features such as hills, promotories, and mountains, in that much effort and energy must be initially expended to situate military forces at such locations, but once attained 'the high ground' can be used to dominate the terrain below with ease. Figure 3 illustrates two-dimensionally the three-dimensional gravity well zones of the Earth-Moon system.During the next few decades military space activities and the development of various commercial space enterprises, or the process of 'space industrialization', will be conducted primarily within this system. Possible military missions to be eventually conducted in the space environment include ballistic missile defence, the destruction of Earth-based targets, the regulation of the flow of space traffic, the defence of military and industrial space facilities, the denial of strategic areas of space (such as choice satellite orbits at Geosynchronous Earth Orbit — GEO — and the various Lagrangian libration points at which objects revolve with the same period as the gravitational Earth-Moon system and thus remain effectively stationary) to enemies and various surveillance, reconnaissance, navigational, data-transfer, command, control, communications and intelligence functions. Figure 4 summarizes active and support military space functions.

Near Earth Orbit (NEO), or aero-space, extends some 50 to 200 km above the Earth's surface incorporating the mesosphere and lower edge of the ionosphere in a zone where ballistics and aerodynamics are closely interrelated. In the short term NEO will remain the primary location for the deployment of manned and unmanned military space systems, and likely space industrialization and research facilities such as current and future Soviet space stations and the planned US-multinational space station.

It is through NEO that ballistic missiles must proceed during their boost and re-entry phases, and are particularly vulnerable to ballistic missile defence systems. However, long-range nuclear blast effects at altitudes between 50 and 150 km are minimal because above 50 km the mechanical effects of shockwave pressures are minimized as a consequence of the relatively low atmospheric density, while simultaneously, below 150 km this atmospheric density remains

Figure 3 The tactical space environment of the Earth-Moon system (generalized and not to scale). L_1, L_2, L_3, L_4, and L_5 indicate Lagrangian Libration points; orbits of stable equilibrium are shown for L_4 and L_5.

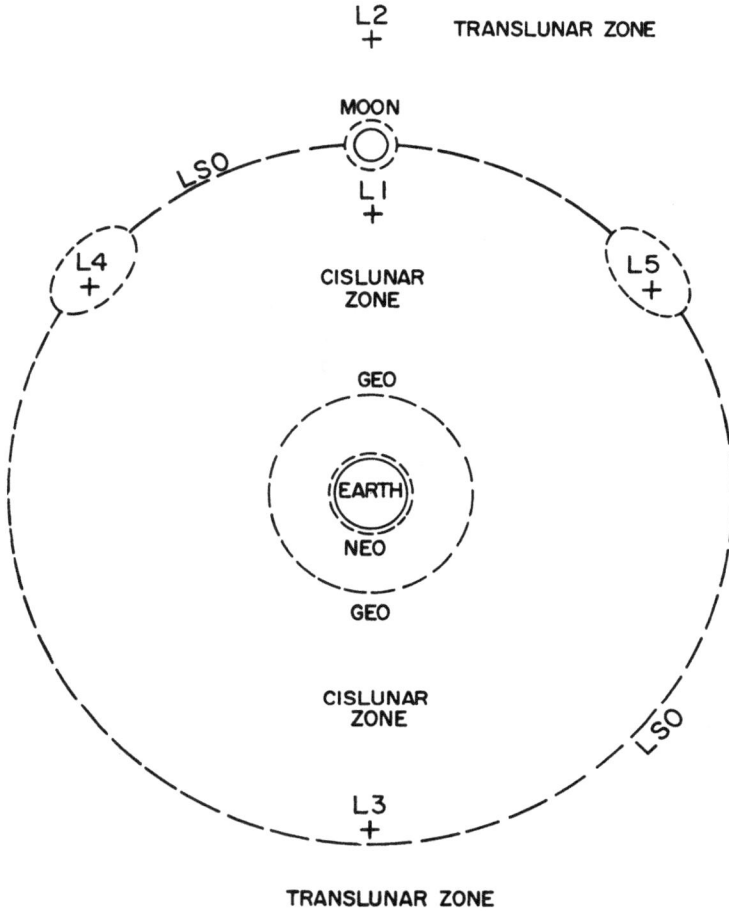

39

Figure 4 Military uses of space

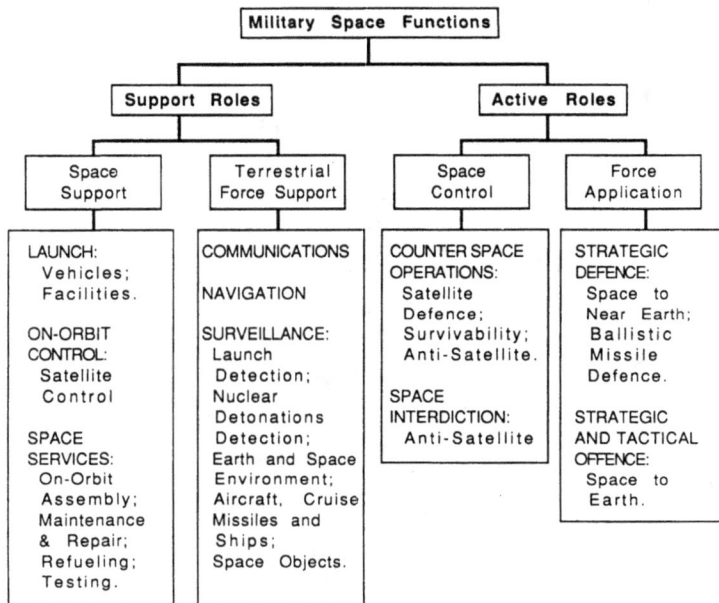

Military Space Functions			
Support Roles		**Active Roles**	
Space Support	Terrestrial Force Support	Space Control	Force Application
LAUNCH: Vehicles; Facilities. ON-ORBIT CONTROL: Satellite Control SPACE SERVICES: On-Orbit Assembly; Maintenance & Repair; Refueling; Testing.	COMMUNICATIONS NAVIGATION SURVEILLANCE: Launch Detection; Nuclear Detonations Detection; Earth and Space Environment; Aircraft, Cruise Missiles and Ships; Space Objects.	COUNTER SPACE OPERATIONS: Satellite Defence; Survivability; Anti-Satellite. SPACE INTERDICTION: Anti-Satellite	STRATEGIC DEFENCE: Space to Near Earth; Ballistic Missile Defence. STRATEGIC AND TACTICAL OFFENCE: Space to Earth.

high enough to reduce the range of corpuscular radiation through dispersion and absorption so that the long-range thermal effect is also minimized. Therefore, even very powerful nuclear weapons in the megaton range must be detonated at relatively close proximity to targets in this zone to be mechanically and thermally effective, although electromagnetic pulse (EMP) effects could seriously disrupt unhardened electronic systems at long-range distances.

Military forces at NEO could dominate Earth-based opposing forces for the following reasons:

1 the greater immediate expenditure of work (defined in physical terms as the result of a force, incorporating the variables of time and energy, overcoming a definite distance) required of Earth-based forces to attack space-based forces; and

2 the inherent advantages that the space environment afford, such as 'look-down shoot-down' capabilities, unlimited interior lines of movement, superior lines of communications to similarly

situated forces and greater manoeuvrability because of lesser immediate work requirements.

For example, an offensive space-based weapon system such as a Fractional Orbit Bombardment System (FOBS) situated at NEO could attack Earth-based targets directly with a minimum of warning time.

However, targets at NEO, compared to those at higher gravity well zones, are relatively vulnerable to Earth-based intervention (in particular directed-energy beam weapons) because of an inherently short warning time available for the implementation of counter-measures and the minimal amount of energy that the enemy must expend to reach this zone. Satellites in such low fixed orbits are also predictably located if they do not have a manoeuvrability capability. Arguments against space-based BMD systems usually stress these factors.

The Cislunar zone has a radius of some 384,000 km and consists of all space between NEO and Lunar Surface orbit (LSO), and includes Geo-synchronous Earth Orbit (GEO) which is located 35,786 km above the Earth's equator. GEO is presently extensively utilized by various nations for the positioning of satellites in an orbit that is stationary relative to the Earth's surface rotation and will take on an even greater significance if space industrialization projects such as solar power satellite systems and other large space platforms are proved feasible. Military forces in the Cislunar zone have the defensive advantage of a longer reaction time to implement counter-measures against enemy interdiction originating from Earth-based forces or space-based forces situated at NEO.

LSO consists of the perimeter zone of the Earth-Moon system where the Moon's orbital path around the Earth is located, and also includes Near Lunar Orbit (NLO), or the space immediately surrounding the moon. The Translunar zone is an intermediate area comprised of the space from LSO to a distance of approximately 1 million km from the Earth's surface where the solar gravity well begins to predominate. These final zones, including the five Lagrangian libration points, will attain increasing military significance as space industrialization, and correspondingly increased technological capabilities, continues. It is possible that strategically placed military forces at the Lagrangian libration points and the lunar surface could eventually dominate the entire Earth-Moon system.

The directions of Soviet efforts in space clearly stem from the long-standing Soviet goal of obtaining superior military forces-in-being and corresponding world dominant power status. Soviet capabilities indicate a desire to control access to, and perhaps deny, the use of space to other potential opponents.

Current Soviet military space strategy and doctrine has the following basic characteristics:

1 Robust launch rates and economies of scale derived from the assembly-line mass production of launch vehicles and spacecraft. Strong forces in being.
2 Integration of military space capabilities in support of all tactical and strategic operations at land, sea, air and outer space. Wide variety of active and support space systems, some without western counterparts. New offensive systems are accompanied by a defensive counterpart (e.g. FOBS and ASAT, ICBM and ABM).
3 Emphasis on 'man-in-space' rather than solely autonomous space systems. Clear goals for the development of manned space capabilities.
4 Exploitation of proven technological systems, but with concurrent vigorous efforts to develop and obtain advanced capabilities. Lack of reliance on 'sole solution' technical fixes.

The Soviet Union continues to launch consistently more spacecraft each year than the combined totals of the world's other space-faring nations (United States, France/ESA, Italy, Japan, and China). In 1986 the Soviets launched 91 space missions carrying 114 pay-loads, somewhat lower totals than previous years, but still more than 90 per cent of worldwide space operations. It is estimated that 70–80 per cent of all Soviet space missions are purely military in nature, while another 15 per cent are partly military.[18] Figures 5, 6, and 7 illustrate the increasing superiority of the Soviet Union in successful space launches, pay-loads to orbit (some launches to orbit contain multiple pay-loads), and total pay-load weight in orbit. It is obvious that the Soviets are outlaunching the United States at least five to one, and placing almost ten times the amount of pay-load mass into orbit. These trends are also illustrative of the decline of US launch capabilities after the Apollo Project, which was accentuated by the space shuttle Challenger disaster in January 1986. A portion of the high Soviet launch rate can be attributed to the launch profile limiting geographic/geometric location of the Soviet Union and technological constraints such as the shorter operational life of its various unmanned satellite systems, compared to more technically sophisticated western systems. However, Soviet satellite technology is steadily improving

Figure 5 Soviet and US successful space launches 1957–87
(Data sources: *TRW Space Log*; US Congress; *Aviation Week and Space Technology*)

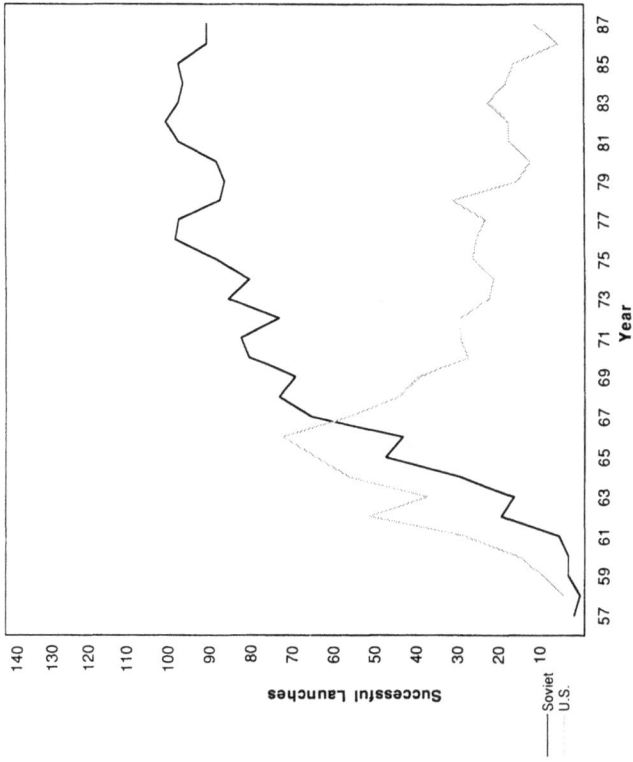

Figure 6 Soviet and US successful payloads to orbit 1957–87
(Data sources: *TRW Space Log*; US Congress: *Aviation Week and Space Technology*)

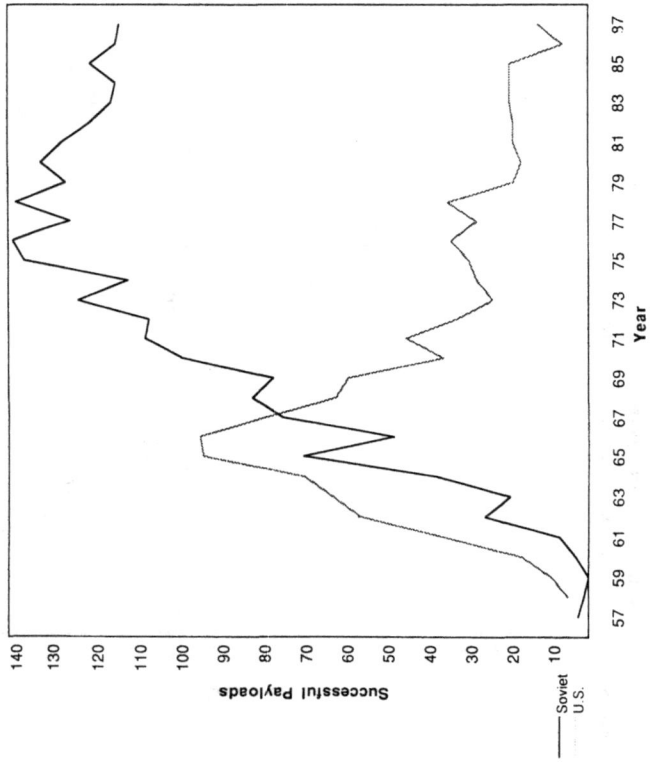

Figure 7 Soviet and US payload weight to orbit or beyond 1957–80
(Data sources: *TRW Space Log; US Congress; Aviation Week and Space Technology*)

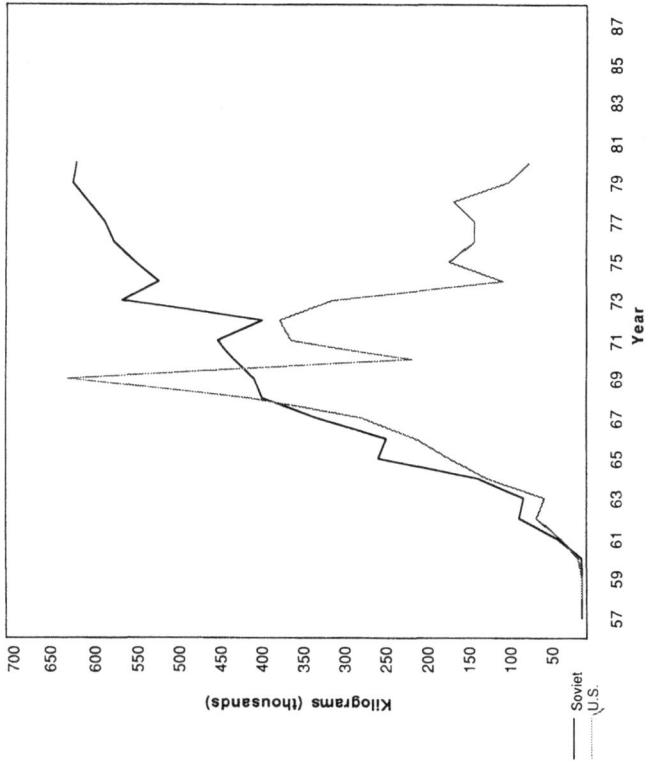

in capability and longevity, and it is unlikely that their vigorous launch capability will be easily forsaken. Rather, it will likely be directed towards other applications. This capability is largely due to the standardization of basic satellite design (in particular the Cosmos series) and launchers and corresponding mass production,[19] compared to the western practice of customized unit and batch production. Proven designs and technological capabilities are exploited to the maximum by the Soviets.

An example of the resiliency of Soviet space capabilities that cannot be matched by the west is typified by a serious incident that occurred on 3 October 1986, when a SL-6 booster (original Vostok launcher derivative) malfunctioned and placed a missile warning satellite into a useless orbit.[20] The Soviets quickly recovered by successfully using the same type of booster to launch another missile warning satellite only twelve days after the mishap. Other similar prompt recoveries have been made after setbacks to the Soviet manned programme, in stark contrast to the prolonged debilitating effect on the American space programme as a result of the space shuttle Challenger disaster.

Whether Soviet planners view space merely as a theatre of military operations, analogous to sea control, or an arena with its own intrinsic value is debatable.[21] There is no doubt that a paced, methodical, typically Russian approach is being taken to integrate space capabilities within the Soviet combined arms doctrine of total force integration.[22] US intelligence sources believe that Soviet military space doctrine aims 'to attain and maintain military superiority in outer space sufficient both to deny the use of outer space to other states and to assure maximum space-based support for Soviet offensive operations', and since the ability to provide support from space for combat operations on Earth requires freedom to operate in, and preferably dominate space, 'Soviet military doctrine fully recognizes the decisive need to disrupt, if not destroy, enemy command, control and communications assets'.[23]

A recent focus of Soviet military space efforts has been the provision of direct support for terrestrial operations.[24] The major elements of this support have been:

1 Target location, identification and characterization.
2 Order of battle data.
3 Force deployment/manoeuvre monitoring.
4 Situation assessment.
5 Geodetic information for tactical nuclear targeting.

6 Mapping and positioning.
7 Communications.
8 Meteorological support.

Such areas of space support provide real-time assistance for the accomplishment of ground-based tactical/operational missions. For example, it is believed that Soviet advisers have used space assets to assist Egyptian planners during the 1973 Arab-Israeli War, to plan and conduct combat operations in Afghanistan, and to monitor US military exercises around the world. The overall Soviet military force structure is also moving in a direction that will make it more dependent upon space assets for C^3I and other strategic functions: a capability and willingness to project forces beyond the Eurasian landmass; growing long-range bomber and SLBM submarine fleets; and a sea-control rather than strictly sea-interdiction role of the Soviet Navy.

The integration of Soviet military space systems into their overall strategic force structure was evidenced by an integrated test of offensive and defensive systems and C^3I systems during a seven-hour period on 18 June 1982.[25] In this short period of time, the Soviet military orchestrated the firing of two SS-11 ICBMs from operational silos, followed very shortly by the launch of an intermediate range SS-20 missile from an operational site, an anti-satellite (ASAT) test against a target in space, a SLBM launch, and two ABM intercepts against ICBM target vehicles. This test demonstrated in logical sequence, for the first time, all the elements necessary for a coordinated first-strike or counter-force nuclear attack on the United States and western Europe, including the capability to destroy US reconnaissance spacecraft in NEO and ballistic missile defence against a retaliatory response. The destruction of such US reconnaissance spacecraft would make it impossible for the United States to detect time-urgent targets and to determine which enemy ICBMs have been launched and which still remain in silos as targets for a responsive retaliatory attack. The SLBM launch from a Delta submarine in the White Sea represented a follow-on second strike that could be used against cities or in concert with the initial ICBM strike to destroy US bomber bases. This exercise also demonstrates the capability to fight a protracted nuclear war even after an initial counter-force strike.

As of 1985 the Soviets have totalled 98,385 crew-hours in space, compared to only 41,460 for the United States.[26] This manned spaceflight experience combined with emerging heavy-lift launch capabilities will enable the Soviets to develop manned space stations and transportation capabilities that can be turned to direct military application with little modification.[27] A large manned orbital capability would facilitate the research and development of a simpler, but perhaps equally effective, 'man-in-the-loop' solution to space-based BMD and other military systems, compared to individually superior automated US systems.

Emerging Soviet military technologies, discussed in later chapters, include a heavy-lift launch vehicle (HLV); a medium-lift launch vehicle (now believed to be operational); separate large and small space shuttle designs; large, modular space stations; and a new generation of directed-energy weapons systems for ASAT and BMD applications.

OPERATIONAL MILITARY SPACE SYSTEMS

Fractional Orbit Bombardment System (FOBS)

The idea of placing nuclear weapons in orbit is not new, and was probably seriously considered even before Sputnik I was launched. As author Tom Wolfe has so aptly chronicled, many Americans were 'genuinely convinced that the Soviets would send up space platforms from which they could drop nuclear bombs at will, like rocks from a highway overpass'.[28] These fears were to an extent justified when on 3 November 1967, US Defense Secretary Robert S. McNamara announced that a Soviet nuclear-armed de-orbital satellite designed specifically as an offensive weapon against targets within the continental United States was scheduled to become fully operational by 1968.[29] This weapon system became known as a Fractional Orbit(al) Bombardment System (FOBS). A primary purpose of FOBS was believed to be aimed at delivering a crippling first-strike blow against US Strategic Air Command bomber bases, in preparation for a conventional ICBM follow-up attack against cities.[30]

A total of some eighteen FOBS tests were conducted under the ubiquitous Cosmos banner, between 1966 and 1971, and were of grave technical and political concern to the west.[31] It is not believed nuclear warheads were actually carried in the tests. The basic concept is to launch a nuclear device into a low orbit of some 160 km, slow it down via retro-rockets so that the nuclear warhead(s) will fall on the target(s) before the completion of the first orbit. Theoretically because the FOBS does not complete multiple orbits, the concept is not in violation of the 1967 'Treaty on Principles Governing the Activities of the States in the Exploration and Use of Outer Space, including the Moon and Other Celestial Bodies'. In fact, the existence of this system is contrary to the intended spirit, if not the letter, of the Treaty which prohibits orbital weapons of mass destruction. The first successful FOBS test occurred in January 1967, two days before the ratification of the Treaty between the Soviet Union and United States. The basic military advantage of the concept is that of a 'global missile', thus allowing western targets to be attacked via the South Pole by travelling three-quarters of the way around the world, instead of the conventional North Pole route which is closely monitored for an ICBM attack. In a FOBS attack via the standard ICBM North Pole route only three to four minutes warning time would be provided because of its depressed trajectory, compared to fifteen to thirty minutes for an ICBM attack. It is claimed that a disadvantage of the system is reduced accuracy pay-load; (1–10 megaton nuclear device, reduced from the SS-9's 20–25 megaton capacity in the ICBM mode), and although it did force the west to deploy more complex sensors such as over-the-horizon (OTH) radar systems. It is believed that FOBS employs inertial reference systems with accurate, low-drift gyroscopes, although targeting data could also be transmitted by radio from Soviet fishing trawlers along approach routes! However, all tests were launched on flight paths that scrupulously avoided the United States. Although the Soviets had initially touted the short-lived SS-10 Scrag ICBM as an orbital weapons carrier, it now appears that all of the operational tests were conducted by the SS-9 Scarp ICBM launcher from Tyuratam. Versions of the versatile SS-9 are also used for various other military space applications such as ASAT and ROR-SAT carriers. Several FOBS tests were possibly related to 'space mine' (a form of co-orbital ASAT) developments.

In his 1970 book *War and Space* Robert Salkeld had raised some key issues in regards to the Soviet FOBS deployment:[32]

1. With improved guidance systems and accuracies and larger or multiple (MIRV) warheads, FOBS could mature as a counter-force threat to 'hardened' military targets such as ICBM silos. If nuclear submarines can be located, these could also be targets for an advanced FOBS.

2. FOBS are considered by the Soviets to be strategically equivalent to deploying missiles just outside a country's borders, from which an attack could also be launched with comparably short warning. (For example the controversial deployment of

Pershing 2 missiles in western Europe by the United States is considered by the Soviets to be a threatening action with a pre-emptory capability.)

3   The Soviets have, during the 1950s and 1960s, boasted of developing very large nuclear weapons — 100 megatons plus. A 58-megaton bomb was actually tested in the fringes of near-orbital space on 1 September 1961 (the largest nuclear explosion to date). Such super-weapons, exploded in NEO, could be used as incendiary devices to scorch the surface of the Earth below, and are a natural pay-load for a FOBS.

4   Soviet FOBS tests may have been a pre-cursor technological test-bed for the development of much larger orbital bombs with improved accuracy derived from advancing technology. Such a development could be achieved covertly with few tell-tale signs. Eventually systems could be stationed in deep space.

5   The view that an object is not in orbit unless it has completed a full Earth circuit is technically unsound. Hence, FOBS is a true technical violation of the 1967 Outer Space Treaty.

It is not currently believed that the Soviet Union or United States have actually developed or tested Multiple Orbit Bombardment Systems (MOBS), in which bomb-carrying satellites would be placed in orbits high enough to avoid natural decay and re-entry, and would remain in space until commanded to de-orbit and destroy terrestrial targets. While the United States has not attempted to develop such weapons recent USAF studies have explored an orbital basing mode for the MX Peacekeeper ICBM.[33] Certainly, such an orbital basing could also be achieved by the Soviet SS-18 and other ICBMs. In addition, some observers have speculated that recent tests of an unmanned, miniature Soviet space shuttle prototype are related to the development of a manoeuvrable, orbital weapon system designed to deliver nuclear weapons against US naval forces.[34]

Little is known on the current status of the FOBS programme, whether the Soviets consider the system operational or have scrapped it. However, Article VII, paragraph 2(c), 'Second Common Understanding' of the unratified SALT 2 Treaty states that the Soviets have eighteen FOBS launchers at Tyuratam, and that these would no longer be operational if the Treaty came into effect (six launchers may be converted into launchers for testing missiles undergoing modernization). The United States no longer abides by the provisions of SALT 2. While the current massive Soviet ICBM Force makes FOBS less attractive, if future overall strategic forces levels are reduced as a result of technological change (that is an effective US BMD system) or the political arms reduction process, orbital offensive weapons could again become more appealing to the Soviets. A FOBS system could also be revived to counter by surprise attack the ground-based elements of a deployed American BMD system.

Anti-Satellite Systems (ASAT)

The Soviet ASAT development programme may have begun as early as 1963, although actual testing of interceptors against targets did not begin until 1967.[35] In 1964 the PKO division ('Protivo-Kozmicheskaya Oborono' or, literally, 'anti-cosmic defence') of the PVO-Strany strategic defence forces was established, being charged with the mission of 'destroying the enemy's cosmic means of fighting'.[36] While Soviet ASAT developments are a defensive complement to the offensive FOBS, to a large extent the Soviets were also reacting to the US ASAT programmes of the period: the US Army's Nike Zeus at Kwajalein Atoll from 1963 to 1967, and the USAF's Thor at Johnston Island from 1964 to 1975.[37] Soviet ASAT research and development has also closely resembled that proposed for the abandoned US SAINT (Satellite Intercept) Programme.

James E. Oberg has described the current Soviet ASAT system as 'one of the most underrated and misreported space systems in history'.[38] Critics of this system claim that it is an awkward weapon of questionable military utility, being clearly technically inferior and less flexible than the new US F-15-launched miniature ASAT (and in fact vulnerable itself to the US ASAT, and its radar to spoofing). However, by the end of 1982, twenty tests had permitted the Soviets to develop an operational system capable of intercepting and destroying enemy satellites at orbits of up to at least 2,400 km. The US system is still in the test stage and is politically uncertain.

There appears to have been two distinct Soviet ASAT programme test series: 1968–71 and 1976–82.[39] The system was initially operational by 1971. The first series involved a radar homing satellite that used two forms of co-orbital interception. In one form the interceptor co-orbited with the target, allowing time for inspection before demonstrating the simulated destruction of the target. In the second form of interception the ASAT approached the target using an elliptical orbit at 400 m/sec., thus allowing only a quick inspection before simulated target destruction. Target destruction is achieved in practice either by shrapnel or the vectored ejection of pellets. Until 1976

51

no actual target was destroyed, but simulations were conducted with the interceptor blowing up at a safe distance from the target satellite. Interception was usually achieved about one and a half hours after launch, although during April 1971 and April 1976 the ablity to intercept during the first orbit and within one hour was demonstrated. The first test series was fairly successful, with four complete successes out of seven attempts. The second series of tests beginning in 1976 incorporated two notable changes. A 'pop-up' intercept was developed for quick interception, with two successes out of five attempts. Furthermore, a new advanced optical-thermal tracking system was tested, but was not believed to have been successfully developed during its trial series. It is now believed that the operational Soviet ASAT employs the standard two-orbit radar-guided system. A number of systems are kept on permanent alert at Tyuratam and Plesetsk (snow is immediately cleared at all times from these launch pad sites), and each system employs the standard SS-9 military booster for which there are possibly hundreds of underground silos across the Soviet Union. The actual launch of a Soviet ASAT takes less than ninety minutes from the start of preparation activity.[40]

The present Soviet ASAT threatens only low-earth orbit photo-reconnaissance, electronic intelligence, meteorological, and navigation (Transit) satellites, the manned US space shuttle and, in the future, the US space station. It is not a demonstrated threat to the various US early warning and western communications satellites at 36,000 km orbit at GEO. In addition, the number of NEO satellites in range will decline as future US weather, navigation (Navstar), and communications (Milstar) systems will be located at much higher orbits. However, it should be appreciated that although the Soviets have not demonstrated the ability to destroy a manoeuvring satellite, in some respects it is more difficult to intercept and destroy satellites in low orbits, compared to higher orbits, because as altitude decreases the target satellites move faster in relation to the Earth's surface.

It is indeed possible that the current Soviet ASAT vehicle could be mated to a more powerful booster such as the veteran Proton or new medium launch vehicle to attack space assets at GEO,[41] although this rather cumbersome approach would take at least six hours to execute and would provide ample opportunity for enemy counter-measures. In addition, existing Soviet nuclear-armed ICBMs and Galosh ABMs could be employed to destroy GEO (and NEO) satellites in a direct-ascent mode.[42] Although not specifically tested, the Soviets are technically very capable of launching a small nuclear weapon to geo-stationary orbit in direct ascent within a sufficient lethal radius to ensure the destruction of a particular target satellite. It is also possible that the Soviets could, or already have, under the Cosmos series placed 'spacemines' at GEO that are covertly armed with projectiles or a nuclear weapon, and could be commanded to manoeuvre near intended targets.[43] Oberg has described another potential Soviet method for attacking GEO targets.[44] In this innovative scenario, a 'hunter-killer' ASAT vehicle would be placed into a retrograde geo-synchronous orbit (east to west instead of west to east, the direction the Earth and GEO satellites both rotate) via an energy-multiplying lunar flyby. Once in this backward orbit, the single ASAT could meet all on-coming satellites at GEO head on, destroying them individually with miniature homing missiles, or simply by a single large cloud of pellets. All GEO assets could as a result be destroyed within twelve hours.

Although their operational ASAT has not been tested since 1982, the Soviets could be conducting other ASAT-related missions. Cosmos 1603 launched on 28 September 1984, and now believed to be a new-generation electronics intelligence satellite, exhibited significant ASAT potential because of its extensive evasive manoeuvring capability.[45] Cosmos 1603 executed three energy-intensive orbital plane changes and one altitude change, which indicates significant offensive and defensive war-fighting capability.

Earlier, the Cosmos 1267 expansion module which docked with Salyut 6 in June 1981 was suspected by the Americans to be equipped with clusters of miniature ASAT infra-red homing vehicles.[46] These reports were vigorously denied by the Soviets and never fully confirmed in the west, but do tend to lend credence to the military potential of the Soviet manned space station programme.

It has been speculated that the Soviets could deploy a space-based laser ASAT by the late 1980s or early 1990s,[47] and have already conducted ASAT tests with ground-based lasers, possibly even blinding US reconnaissance satellites.[48] The ground-based laser facilities are believed to be located at Sary Shagan, and possibly Semipalatinsk, and could be composed of several multi-megawatt carbon dioxide lasers. Turnill relates that the apparently unsuccessful Cosmos 1174 ASAT test of April 1980 using an optical-thermal target detection system may have also employed a laser weapon in an attempt to disable a target satellite.[49] Others claim that in 1983 the Salyut 7 space station was configured as a tracking target for ground-based anti-satellite lasers, and the cosmonauts on board were routinely ordered to put on protective goggles when overflying the Soviet territory where these devices were apparently located.[50]

A first-generation Soviet space-based laser ASAT system would probably have only a limited NEO multi-target lethality, but could present a profound political challenge to the west. It is possible that manned platforms could be used for the systems, given the Soviet space strategy that emphasizes manned operations. This raises the challenging possibility of the necessity of destroying Soviet-manned spacecraft in order to defend unmanned satellites against attack. These technologies are closely related to ballistic missile defence and are discussed in more detail in Chapter 5.

Other potential Soviet ASAT developments could include an air-launched system, similar to the current US system, that would use the Backfire bomber as the launch platform.[51] In a different approach, the Soviets almost certainly have developed electronic warfare (EW) techniques to jam or indirectly disable satellites.

Francis X. Kane has outlined the strategic motivations behind Soviet ASAT developments.[52] These are in keeping with the Soviet space strategy previously discussed. A primary motivation is that by attacking satellite systems which support US strategic forces, the options of US 'launch-under-attack' or 'launch-on-warning' strategies are seriously degraded. Soviet ASAT capabilities and development activities provide the following strategic options:

1 Degradation of the US ability to respond to attacks.
2 Employment of ASATs at lower than strategic levels of conflict.
3 Provision of a general threat that is not well understood.
4 Employment against direct-broadcasting satellites that present a perceived ideological threat.
5 Continuing research and development to improve future ASAT capabilities, while maintaining current operational capabilities.

Ocean surveillance satellites

The Soviets have been very active in developing satellite methods to monitor and target worldwide western naval units. The main systems that have been developed for this are the Radar Ocean Reconnaissance Satellite (RORSAT) and the Electronic Ocean Reconnaissance Satellite (EORSAT).[53] The RORSAT programme began in 1967 and EORSAT in 1974. Both generally work in pairs, with each system interchanging data for detailed observations. The United States considers these to be a serious threat to their aircraft carrier battle groups, and consequently RORSATs and EORSATs would be prime wartime

US ASAT targets. The RORSAT and EORSAT systems provide a real-time tactical targeting capability for anti-ship cruise missiles, with direct satellite-to-fleet target co-ordinate data transfer.[54] Each system usually functions for several months. RORSAT actively locates naval vessels with radar, while EORSAT passively detects radio and radar electronic emissions from ships. Any enemy ship attempting to use electronic countermeasures to frustrate RORSAT could give away its position to EORSAT. Both are launched by the SS-9 to very low orbits of 250–260 km and have small engines for station-keeping. In 1986 two RORSATs and three EORSATs were launched, similar to the 1985 launch rate but with more diverse individual flight profiles.

RORSATs use a nuclear-powered active radar system to scan the ocean surface and produce at least 'blob type' all weather imagery (40 metre resolution) of enemy ships. It is not believed to employ high-resolution synthetic aperture radar (SAR). However, some analysts believe the system may have the capability to detect subtle wave patterns set up by the passage of submarines hundreds of metres below the ocean's surface, thus threatening the credibility of the western SLBM deterrence force.[55] These systems were actually used to monitor the Royal Navy during the Falklands War. There is no direct western counterpart to RORSAT, although the United States is becoming increasingly interested in space-based radar and nuclear power systems.

RORSAT is powered by a Ramashka or Topaz-type thermionic nuclear reactor, producing a power output of 5–40 KWe. When functioning properly, after shutdown the reactor is separated from the rest of the spacecraft and boosted to a higher, safer orbit at 950 km, where perhaps some day it could eventually be retrieved. Controversy was created in 1978 when a RORSAT, Cosmos 954, malfunctioned and spread radioactive debris over northern Canada. A second accident with Cosmos 1402 in 1982 resulted in the reactor and fuel being consumed during re-entry over the Indian Ocean and South Atlantic. Subsequently, after some design modifications, RORSAT missions resumed. The growing number of radioactive satellites and amounts of space debris in orbit, largely Soviet, poses a growing threat to other spacecraft and the purity of the Earth's environment,[56] but the Soviets are unlikely to relinquish any military capabilities because of this.

RORSAT and EORSAT will likely see incremental technical improvements well into the future. EORSATs will benefit from microelectronic advances. Technology applied to RORSAT could include that demonstrated by the Cosmos 1500 oceangraphic satellite launched during September 1983, that employed a high-resolution side-looking SAR.[57] Space-based SAR systems will permit cloud coverage penetration over water and land, and will provide significant tactical and strategic capabilities. State-of-the-art SAR systems were developed by the Soviets for the 1983 Vega probe to Venus. It has been speculated that advanced SAR satellites can discriminate underwater features to great depths and detect moving objects. Other space-based sensors for this purpose could include laser-imaging and infra-red heat-detection systems. Such a capability would have a profound impact on the ability of the Soviets to conduct anti-submarine warfare, and would call into question the security of the west's submarine-based nuclear deterrent.

Reconnaissance satellites

Traditional Soviet photographic reconnaissance satellites launched under the Cosmos designation have been identified with a good degree of confidence because of their characteristic altitudes of 100–200 km, and recovery from orbit after a maximum of fourteen days.[58] Until 1968 most of these satellites had orbital lifetimes of only eight days, but a subsequent generation had orbital lives of up to thirteen days. The introduction of satellite orbital manoeuvrability increased the capability of reconnaissance satellites to achieve precise coverage of specific areas. By 1975 Soviet reconnaissance satellites launched in 67 degree orbits had twenty- to thirty-day life spans and were the first generation of Soviet endurable photographic reconnaissance satellites. Many of these systems appear to be modified versions of man-rated spacecraft such as Vostok and Soyuz.

Current generation Soviet reconnaissance satellites have more than 200-day life-spans, and this longevity is steadily increasing to western standards. Many of these military satellites have also performed civilian Earth resource missions, as has the Soviet manned space station programme. For example, the second Salyut 6 crew collected more than 20,000 multi-spectral photographs of varying regions of the Earth, and some 90 per cent of these were supposedly related to Earth-resource management.

During times of international crisis, the number of Soviet reconnaissance satellites launched has increased dramatically compared to the routine launch rate, obviously to obtain detailed coverage of the areas concerned. For example, in 1983 the Soviets conducted intense surveillance of the Iran-Iraq war, Lebanon and the Middle East, and the US invasion of Grenada. During the 1982 Falklands War photographic reconnaissance satellites, RORSATS, and EORSATS were orchestrated by the Soviets to monitor the conflict and, possibly, provide ship-targeting information to Argentina.[59]

Technically, Soviet systems are increasing in longevity and sophistication, although not at the expense of a high launch rate. Digital transmission of imagery is supplementing the traditional film-return method via a re-entry vehicle. During 1986 some twenty-six military reconnaissance satellites, about the same number as 1985, were launched compared to no successful US reconnaissance satellite missions.[60] The increasing numbers of Soviet reconnaissance systems operating concurrently are indicative of the maturity of Soviet command and control of these systems. For the first time during the over two decades old Soviet photographic reconnaissance programme, at least one satellite was in orbit at all times during 1985. During 1986 and 1987 the Soviets suffered several notable reconnaissance satellite failures (Cosmos 1714, Cosmos 1767, and Cosmos 1813), but without an apparent degradation of overall capabilities.

New and emerging technical capabilities include: advanced imaging reconnaissance satellites relaying near real-time digital imagery via a GEO relay satellite, similar in concept to the USAF Satellite Data System Spacecraft that works in conjunction with the US KH-11 digital imaging spacecraft; the ability to store dormant satellites in orbit and reactivate when necessary; increasing satellite survivability and sustainability during conflict; improved satellite manoeuvrability; improved imaging resolution (presently 0.2 to 2.0 metres); and specialized techniques such as the use of beam-splitter mirrors and laser imagery of ground targets.[61] Advanced manned space station reconnaissance and surveillance technologies could involve multi-spectral cameras, solid-state video imaging, and infra-red systems. In addition, unmanned Soviet reconnaissance systems perform civilian Earth resource missions, and are rapidly developing a capability superior to the US Landsat system. This emerging capability was demonstrated with the launch on 25 July 1987 of Cosmos 1870, a 15–20 ton Earth resources/ocean surveillance multi-sensor platform which to date is the largest civilian satellite of its kind placed in orbit. The United States will be unable to match such a large (up to ten times heavier than Landsats 4 and 5, the most advanced American civilian remote sensing satellites now available) multi-disciplinary spacecraft until at least the mid-1990s.

Electronic intelligence (ELINT) satellites

The Soviets maintain two major constellations of ELINT, or 'Ferret' signal intelligence, satellites other than the EORSAT previously discussed.[62] An older system comprises six single satellites spaced in six orbital planes about 60 degrees apart. Each satellite is at an approximate 650 km altitude at an inclination of 83 degrees, completing one revolution about every 98 minutes. Frequent launchings are required to replenish the system. A newer system is being developed at about 850 km altitude and an inclination of 71 degrees, but its final configuration is still unclear. Soviet ELINT satellites are used for monitoring all western civilian and military communications, and telemetry and radar transmissions, and possibly targeting applications.

The previously discussed Cosmos 1603, launched on 28 September 1984, is currently the largest Soviet military satellite ever deployed, and is believed to be an ELINT vehicle.[63] The over-6,000 kg vehicle was launched on the Proton booster, then the largest operational Soviet launch system, marking the first use of this system for placing a single military satellite in orbit. It appears to be a possible component of the new ELINT constellation, and is indicative of a Soviet desire for more detailed ELINT data. The Cosmos 1714 failure of 28 December 1985 also appeared to be a large ELINT satellite of the same type, although at least two others of this series were launched during the year.

Navigation satellites

The Soviets are steadily developing their Global Navigation Satellite System (GLONASS), which is similar to the US NavStar Global Positioning System. The constellation of twelve satellites was essentially operational by 1987. Like NavStar, GLONASS can be used for providing precise locational information to various land, sea, and air vehicles, and potentially for providing pin-point accuracy for ICBMs and SLBMs. GLONASS is located at 20,000 km altitude. There has been some speculation that NavStar could be 'incorporated' into the GLONASS system. The Soviets also launch, on average, five to six smaller tactical navigation satellites to NEO per year, and these systems have a dual navigation/search and rescue mission.

Communication satellites

The Soviets are steadily increasing their C³I satellite capability. They maintain two major military satellite communciations programmes, one for tactical and the other for strategic applications.[64] The launch rate for tactical satellites is very high, for example twenty-seven low altitude comsats in 1986. Many of these are placed to orbit by multiple launches from a single booster. The high launch rate is partially due to the geography of the Soviet Union, the resulting wide dispersal of its forces, and the consequent satellite coverage requirements. Two tactical comsat networks exist. One is for long-range communications and is located at an 800 km orbit, with thirty or more satellites for medium-range military communication. The other constellation is located at 1,400 km altitude with several satellites. The average life-span of these satellites is two years. 'Store and dump' data transmission is employed for a non-real-time global communications coverage. The proliferation and redundancy of these tactical comsat systems makes enemy jamming or direct attack very difficult.

Strategic coverage is provided by the Molnyia One satellite network of eight satellites. The unique 'Molnyia' orbit consists of very eliptical orbits with perigees of 500 km and apogees of 40,000 km. The network is maintained with about six launches per year, and each satellite has an operational life of up to two years. Therefore, this system is also very redundant.

Although the Soviets still emphasize alternative traditional ground-based C³I systems (that is, radio and telephony), space-based systems will increase their global military capabilities. They also currently have commercial GORIZONT, RADUGA, and EKRAN domestic and international comsats at GEO, and these are of comparable technical sophistication to western systems. These Soviet systems could also be used to provide military communications, as can western comsats. The US military predicts that over the next decade the Soviets will develop increasingly advanced C³I systems, some of which might relay transmissions from manned orbital platforms.[65]

Other applications

The Soviets have developed effective military satellites for various other military and quasi-military applications that are comparable to analogous western systems. Such applications include the early warning of nuclear attack, nuclear detonation detection, meteorological analysis (for example the Meteor weather satellite series), geodesy and map-making (important for ICBM/SLBM accuracy), and radar calibration for ABM and space-tracking systems. In 1984 and 1985 a successful major effort was made to reconstitute the Soviet early-warning satellite network, replacing seven of nine satellites in each year. Soviet early warning satellite technology has traditionally suffered due to a lack of sophisticated infra-red sensor systems, which has resulted in a tendency towards an increased reliance on ground-based radar systems. However, capabilities are steadily improving in this area. In general, the Soviets have at least matched the west in all military space applications and are steadily gaining in technical sophistication.

4

The strategic rocket forces

BACKGROUND AND FORCE STRUCTURE

In a sense because every long-range ICBM travels through space during some 98 per cent of its trajectory, these systems are 'space weapons'. ICBM re-entry vehicle warheads are delivered by a highly specialized spacecraft known as a 'post-boost vehicle' which has its own reaction control system, on-board computers, and manoeuvring capability. An ICBM lifts this spacecraft into space, which then manoeuvres to release its re-entry vehicles. For example, the Soviet SS-18 'Satan' ICBM is still in its boost phase at about 100–150 km (and vulnerable to space-based BMD systems) and reaches more than 1,000 km into near Earth space at the peak of its trajectory which is higher than the altitude of 40 per cent of all satellites at NEO. Moreover, ICBM derivatives have traditionally been employed as satellite expendable launch vehicles by the Soviet Union, China, and the United States, and today's powerful systems would appear to have much growth potential in this area. ICBMs can also be employed for specialized space-related tasks, such as the recent indications that the Soviets keep at the ready some 150 ICBMs for chemical warfare payloads, and have conducted numerous recent tests of tumbling re-entry vehicles designed to spray lethal or debilitating chemicals over wide surface areas.[1]

As a result of these factors, and its traditional close involvement with Soviet space launch and other activities, the *Raketnaya Voiska Strategisheskogo Naznacheniya*, or Strategic Rocket Forces (SRF), is a key element of the overall Soviet space programme. This distinct branch of the Soviet Armed Forces is the technological culmination of the historical Russian military keen interest with heavy artillery.[2] This study will be concerned only with Soviet long-range strategic ballistic missiles, although the importance, and growing capability, of other Soviet strategic forces (penetrating bombers, cruise missiles, and submarine launched ballistic missiles) and tactical short-range missile systems is fully recognized.

Little public information is available on the SRF. Originally Soviet ICBM development was undertaken by the Main Artillery Directorate (GAU), later named the Main Missile and Artillery Directorate (GRAU). The GRAU, an agency of the Soviet Ministry of Defence, was also responsible for nuclear weapons development, determining requirements for new strategic weapons systems, and co-ordinating these activities with other elements of the armed forces and the military industries responsible for manufacturing and deploying new systems. The industrial side of ICBM development is under the administrative direction of the Ministry of General Machine Building ('Ministerstvo Obshchego Mashinostroyeniya', sometimes abbreviated as Minobshchemash or MOM). After the Second World War missile development production programmes were originally controlled by the Ministry of Aircraft Production. MOM was split off from this ministry to form a new ministry on 2 March 1965. MOM was headed by S.A. Afanasyev from its inception until 1983, when he was succeeded by O.D. Baklanov. MOM has four Main Production Units ('Glavnoye promyshlennosti upravleniye', or GPU): strategic missiles and space vehicles; propulsion; guidance; and ground and support equipment. The Strategic Missiles and Space Vehicles GPU may have responsibility for both military and civilian space vehicles.

Basic research and development related to ICBM development is undertaken by various institutes of the Soviet Academy of Sciences and research establishments of the Ministries of Defence and General Machine Building. The first stage in ICBM development is the development of a tactical technical task document ('Taktiko-tekhnicheskoye zadanie' or TTZ) by the Ministry of Defence and MOM. The TTZ outlines the objectives of the ICBM programme with a corresponding work schedule, and initiates the scientific-exploratory phase of its development. The principal Soviet scientific research institute associated with ICBM development is NII-88, located in the Moscow suburb of Kaliningrad. NII-88 is closely associated with the adjacent Korolev Design Bureau facility. The actual engineering development of an approved ICBM design is conducted by a design bureau, whose functions also extend into the management and support of missile production. There are currently at least seven design bureaux and five production plants involved in the development of strategic missiles, space boosters, and supporting propulsion and guidance systems.

The Soviets officially stress the constant combat readiness of the SRF[3] which has the overall mission of deploying medium/intermediate-range missiles with ranges of between 1,000 and 5,500 km and ICBMs with ranges exceeding 5,500 km. These forces are described as being

> capable of delivering charges of colossal yield, of covering vast distances, of successfully overcoming anti-missile defence measures, and of delivering accurate and unavoidable strikes against an aggressor, should he suddenly attempt to unleash a war against the Soviet Union and the countries of the socialist community.[4]

It is also possible the SRF has some operational control over Soviet Navy SLBM development and deployment.

The SRF is the newest and smallest of the five armed services which form the Soviet Armed Forces, but is also considered to be the most important of the services by the Soviets.[5] The SRF is the largest missile force in the world, controlling all Soviet land-based ICBMs, IRBMs, and MRBMs. It was established under the auspices of Khrushchev in December 1959 from existing artillery formations that were granted an instant elite status for their special role in the new 'nuclear age'. SRF officers and troops are hand-picked and provided with specialized technical training.

The SRF is commanded by a Commander-in-Chief usually with the rank of Marshal of the Soviet Union (currently General of the Army Maksimov, who is also a Deputy Minister of Defence). He is responsible for the administration and technical control of the SRF, with the General Staff of the Ministry of Defence having responsibility for executing the operational decisions for the SRF dictated by the Supreme High Command (VGK), with the final decision for the use of nuclear weapons being made at the political level by the Defence Council of the Politburo. In addition, the General Staff can theoretically bypass SRF headquarters and directly control these missile forces.

The current SRF order-of-battle consists of some 1,398 ICBMs and 553 IRBM/MRBMs. These comprise six missile armies organized, artillery-style, into corps, divisions, regiments, battalions, and batteries, with 28 field launching areas, 300 launch control headquarters, and three missile test centres. A battery comprises a single ICBM or IRBM/MRBM launcher. Total SRF manpower is about 300,000 personnel.

Generally the ICBM forces of the SRF are deployed in complexes adjacent to the Trans-Siberian Railway, with several ICBM bases in close proximity to major Soviet population centres.[6] From approximately west to east, Soviet ICBM complexes are located at Pervomaysk (SS-19), Derazhnya (SS-11 and SS-19), Kozelsk (SS-11 and SS-19), Teykovo (SS-11), Yedrovo (SS-17), Kostroma (SS-11 and SS-17), Yoshkar Ola (SS-13), Tatishchevo (SS-19), Dombarovskiy (SS-18), Perm (SS-11), Kartaly (SS-18), Tyuratam (SS-9), Imeni Gastello (SS-18), Zhangiz Tobe (SS-18), Aleysk (SS-18), Gladkaya (SS-11), Uzhur (SS-18), Drovyanaya (SS-11), Olovyannaya (SS-11), and Svobodnyy (SS-11).[7] A typical ICBM complex includes a main base support area, a facility for transporting equipment and missiles from rail transport to road transport, and C³I centres. Each complex is comprised of a number of launch groups, which in turn comprise six to ten launch silos.

As discussed in the previous chapter, published Soviet doctrine stresses the avoidance of surprise attack through offensive operations and pre-emptive nuclear attacks effectively reducing the strength of an enemy retaliatory strike, and thus limiting damage to the Soviet Union. The SRF is the primary Soviet strategic force, and would have the wartime task of destroying all enemy nuclear forces (ICBM launch silos, launch control facilities, support and maintenance facilities, strategic bomber bases, submarine berths and loading facilities, and nuclear storage and production facilities), the enemy economy, systems of government and military control, and all military forces and fleets. Priority targets would also include all those related to a military power projection capability such as depots, transportation centres, military stockpiles, and training centres. Enemy capabilities related to conducting a protracted war such as military-industrial production facilities, refineries, electrical and nuclear power plants, and military and civilian C³I centres would also be attacked. The SRF has a secondary role, primarily through its IRBM/MRBM forces, to support tactical combined operations and naval forces.

There is also some indication that emerging Soviet technical strengths in missile readiness and rapid response, and efficient new generation radar systems and launch detection satellites, have given the SRF the capability to adopt a more defensive launch on-warning or launch-under-attack strategy if necessary, in addition to the traditional pre-emptive strategy. Emerging technologies such as sophisticated satellite sensors and C³I and navigation systems could also assist the SRF in undertaking specialized tasks such as *accurately* attacking deployed western naval units with long-range strategic ballistic missiles.

TECHNICAL STRUCTURE

The SRF is steadily maturing in technological sophistication and capability. The Soviet IRBM/ICBM force currently consists of approximately 500 SS-11s (one RV), 60 SS-13s (one RV), 150 SS-17s (four RVs), 308 SS-18s (one to ten RVs), 360 SS-19s (six RVs), 424 SS-20s (one to three RVs), and 50 to 70 SS-25s (one RV).[8] This force will significantly change during the 1990s as the third-generation SS-11s and SS-13s are replaced by fourth- and fifth-generation missiles, in particular the SS-25. The Soviets have approximately 6,400 ICBM warheads, compared to only 2,100 for the United States (which outnumbers the Soviets in SLBM and air-launched warheads). The Soviet warhead force comprises mostly 1 megaton weapons, about 250 weapons yielding between 15 and 20-plus megatons, and approximately 1,000 sub-megaton weapons.

Between 1974 and 1982 some 2,035 Soviet strategic missiles were produced, compared to 346 for the United States. In a typical year the SRF may conduct nearly 500 missile and booster launches of various types. The US military and NATO has designated Soviet surface-to-surface missiles with the prefix 'SS-' and code-names starting with S such as Sapwood, Scrag, Satan, and so on. The actual Soviet designations for most military launch vehicles are not readily available. The general progression of Soviet ICBM propulsion technology has been from storable liquid propellants to the more recent solid propellants which the United States has perfected for several decades. In addition, the Soviets have reportedly developed superhard silos capable of withstanding blast overpressures of 25,000 to 50,000 pounds per square inch. Appendix B contains a summary of past and current operational and developmental Soviet ICBMs and IRBM/MRBMs. To date, the Soviets have developed some two dozen ICBM-class missiles, although some like the SS-10 Scrag appear to have been technical failures and not deployed.

Since the early 1970s and the ratification of the SALT I Treaty, the Soviet Union has pursued an ambitious ICBM modernization programme.[9] By 1981 this decade of investment had resulted in:

1 The deployment of a fourth generation of ICBMs (SS-17, SS-18, and SS-19).
2 The development and deployment of a mobile IRBM, the SS-20, which some experts believe could be modified into an ICBM launcher (the SS-16).
3 Design efforts on an improved fifth generation of ICBMs (SS-24

and SS-25) which were to be flight tested and moved to deployment by the mid-to-late 1980s.

4 The strategic deployment of highly accurate MIRVed ICBMs in sufficient numbers possibly to threaten the survivability of US ICBMs in their silos.

These improved systems have resulted in such increased warhead accuracy and numbers that some analysts fear the Soviets now have a counterforce kill capability of 0.9 probability made possible by factoring two warheads for soft targets and three for hard.[10] In particular, it is feared the US land-based nuclear force (ICBMs and bombers at base) is becoming increasingly vulnerable. Advanced Soviet ICBM capabilities, in particular those of the highly accurate SS-18 Satan Mod 4, could be used in several other ways. A highly accurate, surgical strike could 'decapitate' the US command structure. Multiple protective structure and closely spaced ICBM basing modes, such as the 'dense pack' mode formerly proposed for the US MX Peacekeeper, could be rolled-up by a creeping barrage of detonating, large-yield nuclear warheads. A crude form of boost-phase BMD could employ the 'pin-down' tactic of detonating a series of nuclear explosions above an enemy ICBM base to disrupt and preclude launches.[11] Approximately 10 megatons per minute, during the enemy ICBM launch attempt, detonated below an altitude of 90,000 metres would be required to make a sustained pin-down attack effective, which is likely well within Soviet capabilities. The USAF Chief of Air Force Research and Development, Lt-Gen. Lawrence A. Skantze, is on record as stating that by 1989 only 1-8 per cent of US silo-based ICBMs would survive a Soviet attack (assuming an optimistic 99 per cent reliability for Soviet ICBMs and warheads, the United States would 'ride out' the attack, and no increase in US ICBM silo hardness).[12] In the future, the Soviets may develop a sophisticated space-based reconnaissance-strike system capable of detecting mobile missiles (such as the proposed rail-based US Peacekeeper MX and all-terrain Midgetman) and co-ordinating timely attacks on such targets by employing advanced real-time battle management systems combined with ICBMs and other weapons capable of rapid re-targeting even while in flight. It is possible that a Soviet ICBM counter-force strike could adopt other innovative tactics, such as a massive launch during periods of intense auroral activity in the upper northern hemisphere that could seriously degrade US radar early-warning systems.[13]

However, critics of the 'window of vulnerability' posed by Soviet

ICBMs to US forces argue that the accuracy and first-strike kill probability of both Soviet and US re-entry vehicles, in terms of CEP (circular error probable) and unpredictable bias, may have been greatly overstated.[14] While Soviet ICBM and MIRV technology may be rapidly improving, it is only catching up to the technical level reached by the United States during the 1960s. There is also recent speculation that the yields of individual Soviet strategic weapons, and the resulting total megatonnage of their arsenal, may have been significantly overestimated by the west,[15] and that the Soviets had significantly curtailed their ICBM build-up trends as a result of the SALT I and unratified SALT II treaties.[16]

However, the specific technical capabilities of the SS-17, SS-18, SS-19, SS-20, and the next generation SS-24, SS-25, and SS-18 replacement are generally interpreted as being very threatening by most western intelligence experts. The SS-17 Spanker (Soviet designation RS-16) is a cold launch (ejected from its silo by a gas generator system before its main rocket engines ignite) ICBM with supposedly sufficient accuracy to present a threat against some hardened targets. Like the SS-19, the SS-17 has a variable range-targeting capability and could be used against Eurasian targets as well as North America. The cold launch technique is consistent with a perceived Soviet ICBM reload and refiring capability because it minimizes silo damage. The SRF has been monitored practising this reload capability.

The SS-18 Satan (Soviet designation RS-20) is the largest ICBM ever deployed, similar in dimensions to the SS-9 Scarp, and about twice the size of the US MX Peacekeeper. The cold launching of this 225,000-kg, 35-metre-tall missile must be a very impressive sight indeed! Currently the SS-18 Mod 4 is believed to be the most accurate Soviet ICBM presenting a direct threat to the US ICBM force. It is estimated that the total SS-18 force alone could currently destroy 65–80 per cent of all US hardened targets, using two MIRVs per target, and retaining a 1,000-warhead reserves for follow-up attacks. The Mod 4 carries up to fourteen warheads consisting of four dummies and other advanced penetration aids, and ten 500-kiloton MIRVs. Some analysts speculate each SS-18 has a growth potential to deploy 30–40 actual MIRVs.[17] The high-yield Mod 1 and Mod 3, with SRVs of 27 megatons and 20 megatons respectively, have the destructive power and accuracy to destroy any known fixed target with a high degree of probability, perhaps including all US/NORAD and SAC C³I facilities. The Soviets are believed to be developing a heavy ICBM successor to the SS-18 for deployment during the 1990s. The SS-18 has an excellent potential for military space-launch purposes, such as those currently undertaken by the SS-9, and other future applications yet unforeseen.

The SS-19 Stiletto (Soviet designation RS-18) has an on-board computer, MIRV pay-load and a combined 'fly-by-wire' inertial guidance system similar to that of the SS-17 and SS-18 ICBMs. This computer system determines deviations from pre-programmed trajectories and provides course corrections and changes. The SS-19 Mod 3, along with the SS-18 Mod 4, are the most accurate Soviet counter-force ICBMs. The SS-19 is comparable in size to the US MX Peacekeeper. Unlike the SS-17 and SS-18, the SS-19 employs a hot launch technique in which engine ignition occurs in its silo.

The SS-20 Saber IRBM (Soviet designation RS-19 'Pioneer') is basically the first two stages of the solid propellant SS-16 ICBM (which had limited deployment). It is highly mobile being carried on a wheeled vehicle, and some analysts believe it could be easily converted to an ICBM configuration. Even in its IRBM configuration it has sufficient range to reach parts of North America. Viktor Suvorov has claimed that the SS-20 has a dual ICBM/*ABM* capability,[18] but this unorthodox claim has evidently not been independently verified. However, such dual purpose offensive-defensive missiles have been examined by the United States in the past.[19] The Soviets are thought to be developing a SS-20 successor for the 1990s, the SS-X-28 IRBM.

The current fifth-generation Soviet ICBMs being developed and deployed are the solid propellant SS-24 Scalpel and SS-25. The SS-24 is the Soviet equivalent to the US MX, while the SS-25 is the Soviet version of the proposed US 'Midgetman' Small Intercontinental Missile.[20] The SS-24 is rail-mobile and has the capability to carry ten MIRVs, while the SS-25 is road-mobile and currently has only a single warhead. The SS-24 is a replacement for the SS-17 and SS-19 silo-based ICBMs. A future MIRVed version of the SS-25 is possible, and a sixth-generation follow-on to the SS-24 is already under development.[21] These fifth- and sixth-generation ICBM systems will have much shorter boost-phases through the atmosphere compared to earlier generations, which may complicate American space-based BMD systems such as those being explored through SDI. By the mid-1990s a significant portion of the Soviet ICBM force will be land-mobile and hence more survivable, a trend that the United States is following with its ICBM modernization efforts.

SOVIET REACTION TO SDI

The Strategic Defence Initiative (SDI) is a research and development effort being conducted by the United States to examine the technical feasibility and development of hardware systems for an advanced BMD system primarily oriented against the Soviet Union. This system, if deployed, could be ground and space-based, being comprised of several layers of defensive weapon systems including lasers (nuclear X-ray, excimer, free-electron, chemical infra-red), particle-beams (neutral and charged), microwave/radio frequency devices, kinetic energy weapons (rockets, 'rail gun' electromagnetic mass drivers), and ground-based endo-atmospheric and exo-atmospheric 'smart' missiles. The specific layers of the system would relate to destroying enemy missiles and warheads during: the *boost phase* when missile velocity reaches its terminal value (6–7 km/s); the *post-boost phase* where MIRVs and decoys are deployed; the *midcourse phase* in which all objects released from the ICBM bus travel in space on their ballistic trajectories; and the *terminal re-entry phase* where warheads, decoys, and other penetration aids rapidly enter the atmosphere towards the intended targets. Advanced space-based C^3I systems and target acquisition and discrimination sensor systems (laser radar, neutral particle beams, microwave radar, electro-optical systems) will be used. The ultimate objective of SDI is to provide the foundations for a complete area defence against Soviet ICBM and SLBM attack on the United States and its western allies. Parallel efforts to develop advanced defensive systems against bomber and cruise missile attack (the Air Defence Initiative) and theatre and tactical nuclear and conventional missiles are also underway. American ASAT developments are also directly linked to the SDI. While subject to much technical and political criticism from various parties, the SDI appears to be making steady technical progress in various areas. The United States may opt for the early deployment of elements of an advanced BMD system by the early 1990s, although this will require modification or withdrawal from the 1972 ABM Treaty.

Obviously, the Soviets are opposed to such an effort to negate the massive investment they have made over the past three decades with their SRF. The official Soviet commentary on SDI repeatedly stresses the first-strike potential that would be afforded the possessor of such an advanced BMD system. For example, a counter-force strike could destroy a large proportion of the enemy offensive forces on the ground; the BMD system could then easily defeat the 'ragged' enemy retaliatory response. The Soviets also claim SDI weapons could also directly attack terrestrial targets. Typical of this Soviet perspective are these remarks reported in the 14 November 1986 issue of *Pravda* and attributed to Yegor Ligachev, Politburu member and Secretary of the CPSU Secretariat, and most powerful member of the Party's Secretariat after Gorbachev:

> contrary to contentions in Washington, SDI is a sword rather than a shield. SDI is not a defensive programme, but primarily one for developing qualitatively new types of strategic offensive weapons based on new physical principles . . . . I can say with full certainty that if the United States nevertheless builds its Strategic Defence Initiative system, we shall provide an answer to it as well; and the US vulnerability will increase even further. The Soviet leadership has made this clear more than once.

The development of an effective US BMD system could effect the Soviets by:

1 Directly confronting the Soviet Union with a technology-intensive armament competition in which the United States has distinct advantages.
2 Severely straining Soviet economic, industrial, and technological resources.
3 Severely threatening the basis of the strategic structure the Soviet Union has allocated great resources to over the past several decades.
4 Seriously questioning the claim that the 'correlation of world forces' has irreversibly shifted to the Soviet Union.
5 Forcing a complete restructuring of Soviet military doctrine and strategy.

Soviet counters to the SDI are taking two basic forms: international political opposition and the threat of technical counter-measures. Political opposition is likely to be combined with limited strategic offensive arms concessions designed to discredit the urgency of the SDI.

Soviet public outcries over US attempts to militarize space have become increasingly vocal since the first US space shuttle flight in 1981. Implicit in these charges is a genuine fear that the United States will effectively employ its technological prowess to take the lead firmly over the Soviet Union in using space for military purposes. In August 1981 the Soviet delegation to the United Nations called for a complete ban on all weapons in space, including ASAT and BMD systems. The US space shuttle was branded as a potential ASAT weapon, and legal questions were raised over US astronauts over-flying Soviet territory (while at the same time Salyut crewmen were over-flying the United States several times daily). In a letter dated 19 August 1983, Andrei Gromyko, then Soviet Foreign Minister, pro-posed that the UN General Assembly consider a 'Treaty on the Prohibition of the Use of Force in Outer Space and from Space Against the Earth'.[22] This draft treaty and subsequent similar 1984 and 1985 draft resolutions by Gromyko and his successor, Edvard Shevardnadze, were obviously intended to stifle the impending development of technologically advanced US ASAT and BMD systems through intense international pressure. The Soviets have also recently proposed an international 'Star Peace' programme to promote co-operative civilian space projects such as Earth applications and manned interplanetary exploration, a defensive anti-asteroid shield, and an 'international inspectorate' with the power to make on-the-spot inspec-tions of satellites before launch to ensure that no country deploys weapons in space. [23] Simultaneously the Soviets have been very careful not to discuss their own military space systems and developments. They have indicated that while they feel Soviet-US co-operation in civilian space research and exploration (for example US space-shuttle-Salyut link-up, and joint exploration of Mars) to be desirable, such activities will basically be put on hold as long as SDI proceeds. In addition to these public displays, parallel serious negotia-tions are being undertaken with the United States.

Since the US-Soviet Summit meeting on 19–21 November 1985 between President Reagan and Premier Gorbachev, concessions have been made by both sides in their bilateral Space Talks.[24] The Soviets had previously insisted that any proposal for ICBM reductions be con-ditional on terminating the entire SDI. Gorbachev subsequently exempted MRBMs from that position and in June 1986 proposed the 1972 ABM Treaty be extended for 15 to 20 years. Under this Treaty, BMD research is permitted, but not testing or manufacturing. In July 1986 Reagan reversed his earlier position that SDI was non-negotiable, and made a counter-offer to adhere to the ABM Treaty for seven and a half years. At the Reykjavik summit of 11–12 October 1986, Gorbachev proposed that the ABM Treaty be extended for another ten years, and provided hints the Soviets were willing to alter their strict interpretation of space research permitted under the Treaty. Reagan rejected demands for the curtailment of the SDI as a precon-dition to any agreement on ballistic missile force reductions, such as the rather unrealistic offer to scrap all ICBMs within ten years. In what they consider to be a serious concession, the Soviets made suggestions that 'basic' R & D for space-based BMD systems not be entirely restricted to the laboratory. However, recently Soviet Deputy Foreign Minister Vladimir Petrovsky put forward the position that testing of actual SDI weapons systems 'could only be conducted on the ground'. This somewhat contradictory stance was echoed by Roald Sagdeev, head of the Space Research Institute, who stated:

> On everything concerning testing of components or elements of space weapons, our position is for a total ban. But if it is a question of basic research, then we consider the laboratory, say a space laboratory, as not violating the ABM Treaty.[25]

Apparently, the Soviet position is that fundamental scientific research, in space or on the ground, should be permitted but that a ban should be negotiated with a threshold at the design stage, including mock-ups and models of specific elements of weapons systems.[26] Reagan is posturing to delay serious negotiations until the verge of SDI system deployment. The Soviets can be expected to make some strategic arms reductions if these can provide a period of time in which to accelerate their own considerable BMD efforts. Significant arms reductions will also increase the likely effectiveness of a deployed BMD system. The United States has recently offered the Soviets a timetable for SDI experiments in exchange for information on their BMD programmes,[27] and there are indications that the prospects for parallel Soviet-US defensive programmes have been discussed by both parties.[28] As a result of the inherent strengths of Soviet space, BMD and ASAT technologies, combined with President Reagan's original 23 March 1983 offer eventually to 'share' SDI technology with the Soviets, there must be a publicly low-key but growing faction within Soviet political and military circles favouring a defensive military space race with the Americans. Soviet BMD developments directly point in this direction.

Indications of potential Soviet technical counters to SDI echo those proposed by western critics of the initiative.[29] While some Soviet accounts may stress the ultimate unattainability of SDI, actual Soviet concerns about this programme appear to verge on the paranoid. One possibility is that as a result of their own extensive BMD research and development, Soviet scientists have achieved technological breakthroughs which have convinced them that a combination of ground and space-based systems would have a credible defensive, and possibly offensive, capability.[30] The deployment of an effective US BMD system, even if with less than perfect performance, would cause great uncertainty regarding a counter-force strike for Soviet targeting officers because there would be no means of determining which ICBMs would be acquired and destroyed and which would survive to destroy targets. In a worst case scenario the most stressful ICBM attack a US BMD system would face, given current Soviet force levels, would involve a near simultaneous launch of approximately 1,000 ICBMs armed with some 10,000 re-entry vehicles, or several equivalent salvo attacks. However, there are also indications that the successful interception of Soviet ICBMs during their boost phase could result in radioactive nuclear debris or fused fully armed warheads returning to Soviet or adjacent territory.[31] This factor would tend to discourage such massive attacks through specific flight corridors.

Perhaps the most obvious and economical Soviet technical response to SDI would be an offensive proliferation of existing ICBM, SLBM, cruise missile, and bomber systems. It is hypothesized that such an offensive build-up could be more cost-effective than the defensive system. Soviet ICBMs have the potential to carry many more MIRVs. This ICBM build-up could incorporate advanced manoeuvring re-entry vehicle (MARV), decoy and other penetration-aid developments. Fast-burn boosters (in which a high-acceleration ICBM burns out in a minute or less compared to the three to five minutes of boost phase for current designs) have also been frequently suggested as a counter-measure. Other counter-measures often quoted include spinning and coating missiles with reflective and ablative substances to minimize the effects of laser and particle-beam-directed energy weapons. However, it would be virtually impossible to convert mammoth ICBMs such as the ten-storey SS-18 to fast-burn systems. Similarly adding even very thin reflective or ablative coatings will incur severe weight penalties and consequent decreased pay-loads. The Soviet SS-24 and SS-25 do not appear to be highly advanced fast-burn designed missiles, but do have an increased capability in this area. Hence the Soviets would be forced literally to replace their (CIA-estimated) trillion-dollar investment in fourth- and fifth-generation ICBMs, and with systems that would perhaps be less accurate and carry much less pay-load.[32]

Innovative decoys and penetration aids such as balloons simulating re-entry vehicles or covering actual weapons could be employed in space. Dummy (and supposedly cheaper with simplified guidance systems) warheads and ICBMs could proliferate many targets to overwhelm the defence. Special ICBM launch tactics and counter-measures could include combined launches of ICBMs and dummy missiles, ICBM launches with a wide range of depressed and steep trajectories, and launches with different azimuth directions (as with a FOBS).

A summary of other Soviet technical counter-measures to an SDI-derived BMD system could include:

1   Pre-empting the deployment of the BMD system by piecemeal attack on system components or a full-scale nuclear strike against the United States while still possible.
2   Salvage-fusing ICBMs and using these to attack the BMD system in a direct-ascent mode.
3   The development of an opposing 'twin' BMD/ASAT system that could be used to neutralize the opponent's system. Neutralization could also be attempted with space mines, ground-based directed-energy weapons, and direct-ascent missiles.
4   Destroying or electronically neutralizing key C^3I nodes of the BMD system, in particular if these are highly centralized. Targeting and acquisition optics and radar systems could be blinded by nuclear explosions in the upper atmosphere.
5   Destroying ground-based laser stations, or spraying the space-based fighting mirrors of such systems with light, highly laser absorptive substances.
6   Changing the brightness and shape of missile exhaust flames, which infra-red targeting systems would use to calculate the exact position of each target missile.
7   Concealment of missile launches by the use of smoke or aerosol atmospheric screens. Aerosol and metallic clouds could also be used in space to mask individual warheads against radar and infra-red sensors.
8   Various electronic warfare methods of jamming, spoofing, suppressing, and distorting enemy signals, and equipping decoys with devices which imitate the reflection of laser, radar, and visual signals from warheads.

Similarly satellite counter-measures to increase survivality against ASAT systems could include:

1   Hardening against directed-energy and nuclear weapons effects.
2   Providing satellites with autonomous defensive weapon systems.

3 Developing satellite manoeuvrability on command or by autonomous (artificial intelligence 'expert systems') threat sensors and on-board data-processing.

4 Hiding satellites in very high orbits to make detection and tracking more difficult.

5 Designing 'stealth' satellites to minimize radar, infra-red, and optical signatures.

6 Providing decoys with sensor signatures like those of target spacecraft.

7 Proliferating a network of low-cost redundant satellites; reserves could be hidden in space or quick-launched from Earth.

8 Providing mobile land, sea, and air command centres to minimize the catastrophic loss or failure of a centralized ground-based nerve centre.

9 Using communication wavelengths extremely difficult to jam (for example millimetre-wave or laser systems).

10 Deploying anti-ASAT weapons to guard satellites.

The SRF is undoubtedly technically capable of attempting most of these BMD and ASAT counter-measures. Significant efforts can be expected to safeguard the massive Soviet ICBM and military satellite investment. However, many of these counter-measures will be very difficult and costly to implement, and will in turn be susceptible to counters.[33] The Soviets will likely attempt to match all future US BMD and ASAT developments in addition to up-grading offensive systems.

5

Ballistic missile defence

FORCE STRUCTURE

The Soviets have pursued ballistic missile defence (BMD) related activities for at least the past three to four decades.[1] BMD systems are directly related to various space technologies ranging from launch vehicles to space-based sensors and weapons. There are strong indications that the 1972 ABM Treaty ratified by the United States and Soviet Union had no practical effect towards limiting Soviet BMD developments such as high-energy laser weapons research initiated during the mid-1960s.[2] The Soviet strategy was to profit from apparent compliance to the ABM Treaty by hindering American technological momentum and proceeding to catch up with their own strategic defence efforts — a ploy they would like to repeat today with SDI. While the Soviet leadership may be publicly critical of BMD in the context of SDI, their own BMD efforts are formidable.

Soviet strategic defence is integrated within their overall offensive military doctrine, and has been emphasized as such since the early 1960s.[3] Such defensive systems are necessary to neutralize such attacking enemy retaliatory forces that would remain following a Soviet counter-force blow. At a minimum this would ensure the survival of important centres of leadership and industry and, hence, the survival of the Soviet system and state.

Towards this end, after ratifying the 1972 ABM Treaty the Soviets retained major operational ABM sites surrounding Moscow, extremely dense air defences (currently some 1,200 sites with nearly 10,000 launchers for various surface-to-air missiles, 10,000 air-defence radars, and several thousand air-defence interceptor aircraft), and continued with a major civil defence programme. While these activities were indeed permissible under the treaty, similar American assets were allowed to atrophy. Soviet strategic defence expenditures during the past two decades were perhaps an order of magnitude greater than those of the United States, with some estimates as high as US dollars $150 billion during the past decade alone.

Soviet BMD is the primary responsibility of the PRO (anti-missile) division of the PVO Strany or Air Defence Forces. The Soviets have developed and deployed first- and second-generation BMD systems and are currently developing advanced third- and fourth-generation systems. Such advanced BMD systems could employ exotic directed-energy weapon and space-based concepts, and there are indications that the Soviets are undertaking an effort equivalent to the American SDI. Furthermore, these developments are compounded by the fact that the technical distinctions between air defence systems and BMD systems are rapidly disappearing.

Until very recently the Soviets did not publicly interpret the terms of the ABM Treaty as limiting the research, development, and testing of futuristic BMD concepts, but have currently adopted a narrower interpretative view to hinder SDI.[4] They do not acknowledge their own similar efforts.

While the 'cost-effectiveness' of strategic defences is a major point of contention in the west, the Soviets do not appear to place much value on this factor.[5] The primary Soviet consideration is the damage-limiting mission of defences and, notwithstanding possible technical counter-measures, there is a firm commitment to invest the resources required to accomplish this mission. There is a current widespread belief that the Soviets are poised with the technical capability to achieve a rapid breakout deployment of a massive national BMD system, as opposed to the limited area defences that presently exist. While not technically 'perfect', this national system could be operational years before the United States could field an effective system.

FIRST- AND SECOND-GENERATION SYSTEMS

The Soviet Union has recently completed an operational transition from first-generation to second-generation BMD systems. First-generation systems consist of single-layer defences that employ a variety of mechanically steered radars to guide long-range missile interceptors with high-yield nuclear warheads to destroy incoming enemy RVs exo-atmospherically (in space or at very high altitude).[6] Such defences are vulnerable to high-density attacks and relatively simple counter-measures such as dummy warheads. Second-generation BMD systems comprise a more sophisticated two-layer endo-atmospheric (within the atmosphere) and exo-atmospheric system that uses short- and long-range missiles and electronically steered phased-array radars. First-generation Soviet BMD interceptors include the SA-5 Griffon/Gammon, the SA-10, and the ABM-1 Galosh. Second-generation systems consist of the ABM-X-3 and the SA-12 Gladiator/Giant.

First introduced in 1963, the dual-role anti-aircraft/anti-missile SA-5 was deployed as a BMD system around Leningrad and the Estonian capital, Tallinn. Today, over 1,000 SA-5 Gammon launchers are deployed around some 100 Soviet cities, ostensibly in an anti-aircraft mode. This vehicle's general performance is similar to the US Nike-Hercules air-defence missile. The SA-5 is a two-stage, solid-fuel missile with a rather modest acceleration rate, and a 250 km cross-range and 30 km altitude capability. It is radar homing with mechanically steered radars, and relies upon small wings for manoeuvrability. Overall, its BMD capability is generally judged as modest.

The multi-stage ABM-1 Galosh was deployed during the late 1960s at four launch sites of sixteen launchers each surrounding Moscow. Each launch site is equipped with associated radars and battle management systems.[7] The Galosh is believed to be similar in performance to the US Nike-Zeus, and employs mechanically steered radars and high-yield nuclear warheads. Its range is at least several hundred kilometres, and it also has an ASAT potential.

The Soviets have been steadily upgrading the Galosh system since the mid-1970s through the development and deployment of a follow-on anti-missile system, the ABM-X-3. This modernized system comprises three components: upgraded phased-array radar systems; SH-4 long-range missiles designed for exo-atmospheric intercepts; and the SH-8 high-acceleration missile for short-range endo-atmospheric intercepts. Both SH-4 and SH-8 are based in underground silos to reduce attack vulnerability. The dual-layer system permits atmospheric bulk filtering to discriminate lighter decoys from heavier actual warheads. The system is thought to be at least equivalent to the US Sentinal/Safeguard/Sprint systems of the 1960s. The SH-4 is likely a three-stage solid-fuel interceptor with a range of 300–400 km, perhaps employing either a low-yield neutron or X-ray nuclear warhead, or a high-yield nuclear device. The SH-8 is probably a two-stage solid-fuel missile with a range of about 100 km, armed with a low-yield nuclear warhead. The Soviets are in the process of increasing the sixty-four old launchers deployed around Moscow to the full one hunred permitted by the ABM Treaty to accommodate the new system

The Americans have also charged that the Soviets have deployed, in breach of Treaty, additional Galosh missiles at the Sary Shagan research and development site,[8] but have subsequently removed the Flat Twin and Pawnshop battle management radars of this system.[9] In addition, while the ABM Treaty limits deployment of anti-missile launchers to 100 *launchers* surrounding a city or ICBM field, it is widely believed the Soviets are stockpiling missiles for their BMD launchers which have a re-load capability. The exact capability of the modernized Galosh system is uncertain, although it is believed that during 1961 the Soviets conducted a number of exo-atmospheric nuclear weapons tests to study the performance of their BMD radars in a nuclear war environment, and developed specialized nuclear warheads designed for RV destruction in space by high X-ray flux and other means.[10] The Soviets widely boasted that they had technically solved the BMD problem, and may have subsequently ratified the US-Soviet Test Ban Treaty of 1963 to preclude American advances in this area.

In addition to the SA-5, other Soviet anti-aircraft missiles appear to have at least a limited BMD capability. The SA-10 is believed to be roughly equal in capability to the American Patriot anti-aircraft missile, with only a limited anti-tactical ballistic missile and cruise missile capability. However, the SA-12 Gladiator hypersonic, manoeuvrable surface-to-air missile is widely thought to have a significant defensive capability against SLBMs, IRBMs and, possibly, ICBMs, in addition to its primary anti-aircraft/cruise missile role.[11] An improved version with enhanced BMD capabilities has been designated Giant, and is believed equal to an up-graded anti-missile Patriot. Gladiator/Giant tests against SS-12 tactical missile targets have been recently observed, and with a nuclear warhead the SA-12 could provide a strategic BMD capability. In general, the massive Soviet air-defence system affords the capability to leverage significantly Soviet BMD efforts by providing a basic infrastructure for the deployment of a national BMD system that would not comply with the ABM Treaty.

THIRD- AND FOURTH-GENERATION SYSTEMS

Third-generation BMD systems are multiple-layer systems employing advanced space- and mobile-air-based infra-red sensors, advanced

79

radars, highly capable battle-management computers, and non-nuclear terminal missile interceptors for both endo-atmospheric and exo-atmospheric target engagement. Such near-term systems should have the ability to avoid the self-blinding effects caused by nuclear-tipped interceptors to radar sensors, and should not be as vulnerable to nuclear attack. American SDI research into these areas, including such projects as the Airborne Optical System and the Homing Overlay Experiment, is well advanced. While similar Soviet efforts are not well documented, the SH-4, SH-8, and follow-on interceptors may have an excellent growth potential in this direction. The speculated Cosmos 1267/Salyut 6 experiment of 1981 with space-based miniature infra-red-homing interceptors may have involved the development of a third- or fourth-generation BMD system, with ASAT applications.

Another interesting possibility for third-generation systems is the use of ship- or submarine-based BMD systems. In forward-deployed Arctic positions, systems based upon derivatives of the Kirov-class battle-cruiser or Oscar-class submarine could intercept American ICBMs during the early stage of their flight paths.

Fourth-generation BMD systems are multiple-layer defences that could include both ground- and space-based kinetic and directed-energy weapons of various types. Such a system would likely empha-size the boost-phase intercept, by space-based weapons, of ballistic missiles during their vulnerable ascent through the atmosphere. It is widely believed that the Soviets have long been vigorously pursuing weapons research and development involving lasers, particle beams, radio frequencies, and other concepts, although such SDI-style activity is firmly denied by the Soviets. However, there is growing evidence that such Soviet research is much more advanced than is commonly appreciated. [12]

The Soviets apparently have a very large laser research, develop-ment, and engineering programme for both tactical and strategic mili-tary applications. Such applications include tank and helicopter range-finding, tactical mobile air-defence systems intended to blind enemy pilots and soldiers, and strategic ASAT and BMD systems. Various American defence intelligence estimates cite the Soviet high-energy laser programme as being some three to five times larger than the US effort. [13] However, it is still believed that the west leads the Soviet Union in such qualitative areas pertinent to space-based lasers as: high-performance optical systems; on-board spacecraft computing systems; artificial intelligence/expert systems software; early-warning and electro-optical sensors; electronics miniaturization; and lightweight spacecraft structures. While still subject to much speculation, key highlights of the Soviet laser effort are believed to include:

1   An estimated 10,000 Soviet scientists and engineers in twelve research centres are involved with laser weapons programmes costing at least US $1 billion per year.[14] This represents the largest laser research programme in the world today. However, the particular limitations of Soviet technological development reviewed in Chapter 2 must be recalled when attempting to judge the productivity of this massive effort.

2   Significant strategic laser research is conducted at the Sary Shagan missile test centre in Kazakhstan, where resides one laser believed capable of damaging satellites and another for BMD test purposes.[15] These are believed to be gas dynamic and iodine lasers.[16] It is possible that the Sary Shagan ASAT laser has blinded and/or disabled US satellite optical and electronic systems, and that the flash-initiated, iodine-pulsed laser has successfully conducted tests to destroy target ICBM RVs entering the atmosphere over the complex.[17] It has also been speculated that the iodine laser could also be a particle beam weapon, or even a hybrid laser/particle beam system. There has been no official United States Government confirmation to date of such specific, advanced Soviet laser capabilities.

3   Additional laser development is conducted at the Semipalatinsk nuclear weapons research facility at Azgir in Kazakhstan, at the Dubna research facility near Moscow, and at least two other smaller facilities.[18] Another facility may be located at Troitsk near Moscow which has deployed carbon-dioxide gas dynamic and electron-beam pumped lasers capable of damaging satellites in NEO.[19] There is also recent speculation of new, very large ASAT/BMD laser bases located at high-altitude, mountainous locations in the Soviet Union.

4   The Soviets have recognized that the conversion of energy from pulsed power is a key technology for the development of all types of directed-energy weapons. It is claimed that they have developed a rocket-engine-driven magnetohydrodynamic (MHD) generator which produces 15 megawatts of short-term electric power.[20] Such a compact power source apparently has no current counterpart in the west, although SDI research is likely moving in this direction. A Soviet 'nuclear explosive generator' may also have been developed.[21]

5   The Soviets are pursuing other technologies critical to laser

weapons such as high-quality optical components. The West German Defence Ministry has recently disclosed information that reveals East Germany has participated for years in the development of Soviet high-energy laser ASAT systems, with an emphasis on laser, image transmission, optics, and infra-red sensor technologies.[22] An economic agreement signed by eastern bloc nations in December 1985 has been described as the Warsaw Pact's answer to the West European EUREKA advanced technology initiative, but it also obviously parallels the American SDI.

6 The Soviet laser weapons programme is thought to have suf-fered a major setback in 1986 with the destruction by fire of its only airborne Ilyushin aircraft laser weapons laboratory.[23] This system was equivalent to the USAF NKC-135 laser weapons laboratory aircraft, and could have potential applica-tions for ASAT operations, protection of high-value airborne assets, and cruise missile defence. It could take the Soviets up to several years to modify another Ilyushin transport aircraft.

The projected timing of the actual deployment of Soviet space-based ASAT and BMD lasers has been quite controversial. In 1982 Richard D. DeLauer, Under-Secretary of the US Defense Department for Research and Engineering, predicted that a space-based Soviet laser ASAT system could be deployed as early as 1983 or as late as 1988,[24] and that by the early 1990s the Soviets could have 'a large, permanent, manned, orbital space complex capable of effectively attacking ground, sea and air targets from space'.[25] Recent Soviet technical successes and military developments with their manned Mir space station complex and the successful launch of their HLV booster in 1987 highlight a growing potential to place a prototype laser BMD/ASAT system in space by the early 1990s. While such a pro-totype system would not necessarily be initially militarily effective, it could provide substantial international political prestige for the Soviet Union. A highly effective, layered space-based BMD system could probably not be deployed by the Soviets until near the turn-of-the-century — a time-frame similar for the deployment of SDI. However, paralleling an accelerated early deployment of SDI systems, the Soviets could probably rush a ground-based laser BMD system, sup-plemented by interceptor missiles, to deployment by the early 1990s.

Even less information is currently available on other Soviet directed-energy weapons programmes. It is known that both the United States and the Soviet Union are conducting experiments related to employing nuclear explosions to 'pump' or energize laser chambers that would generate intense X-ray laser beams. The use of such a weapon for *anti-BMD* and ASAT applications in a 'pop-up' ICBM or SLBM mode would particularly suit the aggressive, offence-oriented Soviet military doctrine. Soviet experiments relevant to such developments have apparently been conducted at Semipalatinsk, where nuclear debris has been monitored being vented from underground experiments.[26] Co-ordination of the Soviet X-ray laser weapons pro-gramme is credited to physicist F.V. Bunkin, a Lenin Prize winner from the Lebedev Physics Institute. Bunkin is also closely involved with the Soviet blue-green laser programme for satellite communica-tions with submerged nuclear submarines. The Kurchatov Institute is providing support for the X-ray laser programme and nuclear weapons plasma systems.

Other 'third-generation nuclear weapons' concepts relevant to BMD could include enhanced and vectored microwave, gamma ray, electro-magnetic pulse (EMP), neutron, plasma, projectile, and other con-cepts.[27] The basic idea is to tailor nuclear weapons so that these can deliver specified forms of energy effects that are concentrated in a specific direction, as opposed to first (fission) and second (fission-fusion) generation weapons which produce a wide variety of effects spread evenly over a surrounding area. If the Soviet Union and the United States continue underground nuclear testing, even at levels substantially lower than the 150 kiloton limit specified by the Threshold Test Ban Treaty, it is highly likely that such a selection of third-generation nuclear weapons will be developed and deployed for both defensive and offensive operations.

Unlike the west, the Soviets have a well-established programme for the development of radio-frequency weapons, in particular very high-peak-power microwave generators.[28] Many western weapons systems could be very vulnerable to such weapons which could damage critical electronic components and inflict disorientation and physical injury on humans. A ground-based radio-frequency weapon capable of damaging satellites, missiles, and RVs could be tested by the 1990s. An advantage to the Soviets of such a weapon would be that it would not require highly accurate target acquisition and tracking systems, because its beams could cover broad areas. A currently operational Soviet 50 megawatt extremely high-frequency transmitter, code-named 'Woodpecker', is believed capable of jamming civilian, military, and potentially SDI radio communications links, and is by far the most powerful broadcasting station on earth.[29] It is widely known that the Soviet Union enforces much stricter microwave safety standards than the United States. The Soviets are also rumoured to be actively developing and testing low-frequency 'Tesla'-type weapons that could conceivably transmit large amounts of energy over long distances through or around the earth!

The Soviet Union has also been interested in the development of particle beam weapons since the early 1950s and is believed to be concentrating considerable resources into this area. Past relevant Soviet research in this area has included:[30]

1 Eight successful experiments that propogated electron beams in the ionosphere and in space from Cosmos satellites and from manned Salyut space stations.
2 Joint Soviet-French 'Araks' electron beam experiments in the ionosphere from sounding rockets, in which narrow beams were propogated tens of kilometres into space.
3 Ground-based charged particle beam propagation tests in 1977 at Sarova near Gorki, possibly as a prelude to the eventual development of a ground-based BMD particle beam weapon.

Key elements of the current American SDI particle beam weapon research and development effort are based upon earlier Soviet breakthroughs in the field.[31] These include the so-called 'Dudnikov Source' which supplies negatively charged hydrogen ions, and the radio frequency quadrapole (RFQ) which serves to focus and accelerate ion beams. The Soviets have also developed electrical storage capacitors using water as a dielectric, pressurized to 100 atmospheres, which have significant capacity advantages over storage techniques developed in the United States. Electron plasma generators are known to have been developed at the Institute of High Energy Physics at Novosibirsk which can function as electron injectors after minor modification.

However, the most controversial indications of major Soviet advances towards harnessing a charged or neutral particle beam as a weapon appeared to have occurred during the mid-1970s when USAF 'Big Bird' reconnaissance satellites detected strange unexplained flashes and radiation emissions, somehow related to the recent construction of an unknown, very large facility at Semipalatinsk.[32] Initial interpretations pointed towards the use of small, contained nuclear explosions to power a high-energy particle beam.[33] Several years later similar activity was detected at Sary Shagan, although for both cases no conclusive evidence has been made public. Although some analysts dismiss these reports, and the feasibility of particle beam weapons in general,[34] noted space expert G. Harry Stine has concluded:

It appears that the Soviet Union has made some technical breakthroughs in the particle beam weapon field because the huge facility at Sary Shagan appears to be a charged particle beam weapon powered by Pavlovski magnetocumulative generators. It appears to be a pulsed air-core betatron, which would produce a high density electron beam of an estimated energy of several hundred MeV [million electron volts]. Reports in the open literature indicate that more than a megajoule [a million joules] of energy has been applied to the Sary Shagan betatron coils. If the Sary Shagan beam is also neutralized, the device could operate effectively as a ground-based ABM particle beam weapon because only a few hundred MeV are required to kill an incoming ICBM.[35]

It is projected, based upon current developments, that by the year 2000 the Soviets could deploy a space-based particle beam weapon for disrupting satellite electronics and for BMD applications. Eventually it is also possible, if somewhat unlikely, that space-based particle-beam generators could be used as a 'death ray' to attack population centres with a shower of lethal high-energy radiation — in effect a large-scale directed neutron bomb![36] In fact, the Soviets have proposed a ban on the development and manufacture of weapons using 'charged and neutral particles to affect biological targets'. However, in a related area, there now appears to be evidence that Soviet physicists are conducting research on *anti-matter* technologies for weapons purposes.[37] When interacting with normal matter, anti-matter results in the complete annihilation of an equal quantity of normal matter with the complete conversion of all matter to energy. As such and being rather modest in size and highly lethal, space-based anti-matter particle accelerators could eventually provide the ultimate BMD system.

6

Space operations

OVERVIEW

The Soviet Union has developed a robust launch capability with a complete family of launch vehicles to maintain its diverse military, scientific and growing commercial space activities. This space transportation system now includes a capability, perfected over the years, to place manned and unmanned spacecraft to NEO literally upon demand. Soviet space station activities have demonstrated a gradual evolution towards permanent space habitation complemented by increasing technical sophistication.

In addition to its proven space transportation systems, the Soviet Union is currently developing new advanced technology launch vehicles, manned re-usable spacecraft, and large-scale manned space station capabilities. Soviet propulsion systems, avionics and computer systems, and structural design are all demonstrating technical strides. These emerging capabilities will likely be integrated in the near term with, rather than totally replace, proven technical systems. However, the Soviets will place a growing emphasis on employing more cost-effective means for the maximum exploitation of space. As a consequence of steady technical advances, Soviet manned spaceflight will inevitably venture beyond NEO to GEO, cislunar and interplanetary space.

In total, Soviet space operations are developing increasing military, scientific, and commercial manned and unmanned spaceflight capabilities that the United States and other space powers (western Europe, Japan, and China) will be hard pressed to remain competitive with. This could remain true notwithstanding possible western advances resulting from SDI and rejuvenated planetary exploration programmes.

86

CURRENT SPACE TRANSPORTATION SYSTEMS

Standard launch vehicle

The so-called standard launch vehicle, or 'A' series launcher, is based upon the original 1957 SS-6 'Sapwood' ICBM.[1] While its utility as an ICBM was somewhat limited, it turned out to be an excellent spacecraft launch vehicle. It was the launcher for Sputnik 1, and the Vostok, Voskhod, and current Soyuz series of manned spacecraft. Other applications have included interplanetary, lunar, and other deep space probes, as well as launching Molniya communications and early warning satellites. In different versions it is also designated the SL-3 (Vostok), SL-6 (Soyuz), and the four-stage SL-4 (Molniya). Over 700 of all types have been launched. Upgraded versions could see service into the next century for unmanned military and commercial applications.

The A series is of a rugged design suitable for mass production and rough handling. Transportation to the launch pad is accomplished horizontally on a railway car, after which it is raised vertical in preparation for launch. Maximum pay-load to NEO is approximately 7.5 tonnes, with total lift-off weight being 330 tonnes.[2] Liquid oxygen and kerosene is used as propellant for its sixteen RD-107 first-stage rocket engines (900,000 pounds total thrust), and four RD-108 engines (total of 550,000 pounds thrust) in each of the next stages.

During 1986 versions of the A launcher were used for a total of fifty missions with only one recorded failure,[3] thus retaining its status as the primary Soviet space launch vehicle. Missions of the satellites placed to orbit included such applications as photographic reconnaissance, early warning, the manned Soyuz T-15 docking with the Mir space station, Prognoz robotic vehicle resupply missions to Mir, Molniya communications satellites, spacecraft experimentation (Soyuz TM), materials processing and remote sensing.

In the future, the A series will likely be largely superseded by a new generation of launch vehicles and recoverable space shuttle transportation systems, but could remain employed as a dependable 'DC-3-like' unmanned launcher. The remarkable A series has recently been offered for international commercial launch services.[4]

Proton launch vehicle

While ostensibly of non-military design from inception, it has been speculated that the Proton, or 'D' series, launch vehicle was originally intended to deliver the blockbuster 60 megaton warheads the Soviets developed during the 1960s. However, the Proton was actually first used to launch three satellites, also called Proton, during 1965 and 1966. The four-stage version began operations in 1967, ultimately launching various Cosmos satellites, circumlunar Zonds, Lunas 15 to 24, Mars 2 to 7, Veneras 9 to 16, Vegas 1 and 2, Statsionar communications satellites, and Glonass navigation satellites. A modified version has also been developed to place Salyut/Mir space stations and heavy expansion modules into orbit. Overall, the Proton is one of the most technically advanced, cost-effective, and reliable expendable launch vehicles in service today.

While originally shrouded in much technical mystery, the Soviets have recently released information on the vehicle's complete technical specifications. They are also undertaking intense international marketing efforts to offer commercial Proton launch services. In general, the Proton is roughly equivalent in capability to the now defunct American Saturn 1B.[5] In all, there are three versions of the basic vehicle, all of which employ a six-engine booster to deliver nearly 2 million pounds of thrust. The six tubes surrounding the first stage were at one time thought to be strap-on boosters, but are now known to be integral liquid fuel tanks each with its own rocket engine, and clustered around a large diameter central engine. The RD-253 engines employed use nitrogen tetroxide as the oxidizer and unsymmetrical dimethyl hydrazine (UDMH) as non-cryogenic fuel. In the two-stage version, a second stage with four RD-253s produces 500,000 pounds of thrust, while a third-stage version incorporates another RD-253 for over an additional 100,000 pounds thrust. The four-stage version employs an upper stage with a kerosene/liquid hydrogen engine capable of multiple restarts and a total burn time of over 600 seconds. The three-axis stabilized fourth stage is also equipped with autonomous attitude control and stabilization systems, power generation, telemetry, and communications systems. This latter Proton version has the advantage of being capable of placing satellites directly to GEO without the requirement of a satellite apogee boost motor, thereby permitting the deployment of smaller, cheaper, and less complicated satellites. The Proton is capable of delivering at least 20 tonnes to NEO (200 kilometre orbit) and 2 tonnes to GEO.

During its over two decades of operation, the Proton has proven to be a very reliable launch system. The overall failure rate to the end of 1985, including deep space launches was 13.64 per cent (18 out of 132 launches); out of 58 launches to GEO only one was a failure (1.72 per cent).[6] However, during 1987, at the height of efforts to commercialize Proton, two out of three launch attempts were failures.[7] The initial failure occurred on 30 January during a geosynchronous launch attempt when the upper stage failed to fire and the pay-load separated in a NEO parking orbit. On 24 April a Proton's upper stage shut down prematurely and failed to re-ignite during the first burn of the launch of multiple Cosmos and Glonass navigation satellites. However, with characteristic Soviet space programme persistence, the Proton was placed back into service only twenty days after the second failure.[8] On 11 May a Gorizont communications satellite was successfully launched to GEO on a Proton. The two failures were explained by Soviet officials as being the results of malfunctions associated with an experimental fourth stage that would not be used for commercial missions.

The recent Soviet efforts aimed at Proton commercialization date from 1983 when bids were placed with the International Maritime Satellite Organization (Inmarsat) to launch its second-generation communications satellites beginning in 1988.[9] The economically attractive offer was refused by the United States on the grounds that sensitive American technology would be incorporated in the new satellites and made vulnerable to direct Soviet acquisition. In fact, the competition was eventually won by Hughes Aircraft and British Aerospace. The Soviets have currently enlisted an American firm, the Space Commerce Corporation of Houston, Texas, to market the Proton in the west in co-operation with the Glavkosmos organization. Glavkosmos has called for an end to discriminatory restrictions that now prevent most western satellites from being launched on Soviet boosters, and is offering guarantees that proprietary technologies will be safeguarded.[10] The Soviets believe that Proton can now fill a launch gap created by the recent failures of the American space shuttle and expendable launchers, and the European Ariane. Third World nations, and organizations such as Inmarsat, Europe's Eutelsat, and Intelsat, have been targeted as potential customers.

This move towards commercializing Proton, in addition to other Soviet launchers, satellites, and space station facilities, marks a significant trend towards offering a 'Glasnost' image of the Soviet space programme to the rest of the world. General conditions for a commercial Proton launch have been offered to include:[11]

1 The exact launch price will depend upon a number of factors, such as satellite weight and orbital requirements, and is fixed through negotiations. In general, the typical price for a communications satellite launch to GEO would be about $24 million

(US 1986), and an entire Proton pay-load to GEO some \$43 million (payable in Swiss francs).

2 Favourable launch insurance rates, negotiated on an individual pay-load basis, will be provided by the Soviet state insurance company, Ingosstrak.

3 The satellite will be transported to Tyuratam on a direct Aeroflot cargo flight, with guarantees of the maintenance of the strict security of the pay-load. The customer satellite launch team can be present at all times.

4 Two launch pads, some 600 metres apart, are available for Proton use at Tyuratam.

5 In the event of a launch failure, a replacement launch will be offered at 'advantageous conditions'.

The Proton has a number of additional potential capabilities in that it has been proposed that it could be employed for the future launch of the French Hermes mini-shuttle, possibly because the Ariane 5 HLV will not be operational until at least the mid-1990s.[12] During 1986 there were ten Proton missions, including the launch of communications satellites to GEO, the Mir space station, and Glonass navigation satellites.[13]

'F' Launch vehicle (SS-9 Scarp)

As discussed in Chapter 3, this two-stage launcher has been used primarily for military vehicle missions such as FOBS, ASAT, and RORSAT. Its capacity to NEO is believed to be similar to the standard launch vehicle (up to 7 tonnes), its principal advantage being a more responsive launch capability. It is based at Tyuratam and Plesetsk, and will likely continue to see future service with the development of improved multiple-function upper stages, although it could gradually be replaced by the new medium launch vehicle. During 1986 the 'F' launcher was used for a total of fifteen missions, all apparently successful, and involving the areas of electronic intelligence, geodetic mapping, ocean surveillance, and meterological and oceanographic data gathering.[14]

Other current launchers

The Soviets employ the small 'B'- and 'C'-class launch vehicles for placing light military and research pay-loads to NEO. The B launcher is based upon the SS-4 'Sandal' IRBM and can deliver up to 1,000 kg of pay-load to a 500-km orbit. The C launcher is used extensively and can deliver up to 1.5 tonnes to NEO. It is based upon the SS-5 Skean ICBM. The C launcher is launched from Plesetsk only, and during 1986 had thirty-six missions including the launch of small navigation and store-dump and tactical communications satellites.[15] The Soviets are currently marketing these vehicles for commercial applications.

DEVELOPMENTAL LAUNCH VEHICLES

Medium launch vehicle

The recent medium launch vehicle (MLV), or SL-16 represents the first new Soviet-dedicated space launch vehicle development in two decades. It is also being used as an important modular element of the new generation HLV, small space-plane, and heavy space shuttle which are all believed to employ co-ordinated propulsion system hardware with a high degree of commonality.[16] This is to be accomplished by the MLV being used to launch the space-plane, and as strap-on boosters for the HLV which itself will launch the heavy space shuttle. In addition, the MLV has a quick-reaction launch capability and potential high launch rate that will undoubtedly be used to supplement earlier generation expendable launch vehicles, in particular the Proton. This could have the desired effect of freeing a greater number of Protons for space station support and commercial operations.

The MLV is a straight-stacked three-stage vehicle with no strap-on boosters or external fuel tanks, and stands over 60 metres high. It has an approximate lift-off weight of 400,000 kg, a lift-off thrust of over 1 million pounds, and is believed capable of delivering some 15 tonnes of pay-load to an orbit at 180 km. Roughly equivalent to the US Titan 4 or Saturn 1-B, the MLV was initially thought by some analysts to employ a cryogenic, liquid hydrogen system. However, it is now recognized that it employs a standard Soviet propulsion system based upon kerosene and liquid oxygen or hypergolic storables. By using a Proton upper stage, or a new design, the MLV can place multiple pay-loads into militarily valuable high-inclination circular twelve-hour orbits, or to GEO.

It is now thought that the MLV's development may have initially encountered substantial difficulties. Initially expected to be deployed in 1984, the MLVs first sub-orbital tests did not occur until April 1985. The first orbital attempt occurred on 21 June 1985 with the launch of three small Glonass navigation satellites, but may not have been entirely successful. To the end of 1986 there may have been a total of seven MLV missions, although some of these may have been classified as Proton missions. On 14 February 1987 Cosmos 1820 was launched on a MLV and is believed to be typical of the military-oriented missions this launcher is primarily intended for. One MLV mission of 30 July 1986 involving Cosmos 1767 may even have been ASAT oriented.

Manned-mission applications of the MLV could involve its being the launcher for the small space-plane currently under development, or a Soyuz-like capsule spacecraft. The MLV could permit manned missions in launch-energy-intensive Sun synchronous polar retrograde orbits with inclinations of 96° to 98° for increased global observational coverage. Christened 'Cyclone' by the Soviets, the MLV is now being offered for commercial applications.

Heavy launch vehicle

Soviet efforts to develop a heavy launch vehicle (HLV) date back to unsuccessful attempts during the 1960s to launch the mysterious 'G' class superbooster.[17] Evidence now appears to indicate that in the rush to win the race to the moon with the Americans, the Soviets developed a launcher roughly equivalent in potential capability to the US Saturn V. It is believed that this superbooster suffered three catastrophic failures between 1969 and 1972 and was never successfully launched. Vague descriptions of this early vehicle seem to indicate a compound cluster rocket design with a wide base and four tapering stages. It was to have used clustered kerosene/liquid-oxygen rocket engines, possibly derived from the reliable SS-9 Scarp.

While the United States abandoned its HLV capability with the end of the Apollo Programme and the launching of Skylab in 1973, the Soviets continued their development of a radically redesigned superbooster. A serious effort was made to master high-energy cryogenic propulsion technology.[18] Cryogenic oxygen-hydrogen-powered rocket engines have been used by the United States for the past two decades, and today are routinely used by western Europe, Japan, and China.

By 1981 it became apparent that a new Soviet HLV was in the offing, which became designated the SL-W or SL-X-17 by the United

92

States Defense Department.[19] It was accurately predicted that this vehicle would be used both as an expendable launch vehicle for large, unmanned pay-loads, and as a booster for the manned heavy space shuttle being developed in parallel. Development of the HLV apparently was hindered during development of its advanced propulsion systems.

Earlier predictions were validated after the vehicle's flight readiness propulsion firing tests during March 1987,[20] and the first launch of the system, named 'Energia' by the Soviets, on 15 May 1987 (which also happened to be the thirtieth anniversary of the flight of the first Soviet ICBM, the SS-6 Sapwood).[21] Energia very clearly represents a quantum leap in capability for the Soviet space programme, being the most powerful rocket in history.

The Energia is, in its recently tested base configuration, a two-stage vehicle with four liquid-propulsion strap-on boosters believed to be derived from the new MLV. It is 60 metres in height, a maximum of 8 metres in diameter, and weighs over 2,000 tonnes. With an estimated 8 to 9 million pounds total thrust from its strap-ons and core engines (making it more powerful than the Saturn V's 7.5 million pounds thrust) it could deliver over 100 tonnes to NEO at 180 km, 10–15 tonnes to GEO, 32 tonnes to the Moon, or over 20 tonnes to Mars.[22] While the strap-ons are believed to burn kerosene/liquid-oxygen, the core second-stage powerplant consists of four engines that burn liquid-hydrogen and liquid-oxygen, and thus represent Soviet mastery of advanced cryogenic propulsion technology. It is even possible that the Soviets may have gone one step further than everybody else by employing 'slush hydrogen' fuel, with a denser, snow-like consistency. Slush hydrogen fuel would permit more fuel to be contained in a given volume compared to standard liquid-hydrogen.

The dummy pay-load carried on the 15 May inaugural flight was a side-mounted cylindrical pod of approximately the same dimensions as a strap-on booster and of an estimated 100 tonnes weight. This pay-load pod incorporated its own orbital injection propulsion system, possibly related to a space shuttle test, which malfunctioned and led to the failure of the pay-load to achieve orbit. It is notable that the Soviet media provided live television coverage of this launch and immediately reported the pay-load failure. However, the Soviets rated the overall mission a success.

It is likely that the four strap-on boosters made a parachute-assisted recovery on Soviet territory, and it is also possible that the second stage cryogenic propulsion system is also recoverable. This implies that Energia is an advanced recoverable launch system. It also appears that Energia could be flown with up to eight strap-on boosters, increasing its NEO pay-load capacity to over 250 tonnes (over seven times the capacity of the American space shuttle). In this launch mode configuration the pay-load would be stacked as a nose-fairing-mounted third stage, increasing the vehicle's height to some 100 metres. The exact number of strap-on boosters used will be mission specific and can vary from four to eight.

One of the primary purposes of Energia will be to serve as the launch vehicle for the manned Soviet heavy space shuttle. This is an exact reversal of the American space shuttle development philosophy, which first proceeded with the development of a manned space transportation system and is only now considering the development of new unmanned HLV concepts derived from space shuttle technology.[23]

Energia appears to have been designed for a broad range of military, commercial, and scientific applications. The Soviets will undoubtedly be able to achieve greatly increased pay-load weights to orbit and economies of scale with it. Launch pay-loads could include:

1 Directed-energy BMD and ASAT weapons systems and various other military pay-loads.
2 Manned space shuttles and other spacecraft, such as those required for a manned Mars expedition. An eight strap-on booster configuration could launch a 200-tonne cryogenic booster that could deliver a 30-tonne, Mir-sized transport on a Mars trajectory, along with associated landing and return modules.
3 Very large space station and structural elements.
4 Heavy communications satellites and other pay-loads delivered to GEO.
5 Unmanned Earth and interplanetary applications and scientific missions.
6 Solar power satellite systems equipped with massive arrays of solar cells to produce energy either for space-based industrial production, or relayed to Earth via microwaves or lasers. In addition, huge mirrors could be used to reflect light to cities and other desired areas at night.
7 Various commercial and space industrialization projects marketed internationally under the auspices of Glavkosmos.

Space shuttle vehicles

The Soviet space shuttle programme has been the subject of western speculation and rumour for many years. The misty origins of the programme probably lie with the interest Stalin evidenced immediately following the Second World War in Eugen Sanger's wartime proposals for the development of a German long-range hypersonic rocket-propelled manned bomber that was to 'skip' along the upper reaches of the atmosphere.[24] It is thought by some that during the 1950s and 1960s the Soviets may have conducted preliminary experiments on an unmanned winged boost-glide vehicle.[25] This speculation was fuelled by the Soviet practice of depicting advanced-winged spacecraft on postage stamps and through other media channels. There is one intriguing possibility where this early project may have evolved. The Soviet defector and writer Viktor Suvorov has described a so-called 'Yastreb' pilotless rocket aircraft that is supposedly used by the Soviets for photographic and electronic reconnaissance at heights of more than 30 kilometres and at speeds in excess of 3,500 kilometres per hour.[26] Suvorov also indicates that the Yastreb could be used as a strategic bomber.

By the late 1960s the Soviets probably began the development of specific manned space shuttle projects. Their motivation was undoubtedly the same as that which rationalized American space shuttle development: decreasing costs through the use of re-usable hardware and increasing manned spaceflight capabilities. It is believed by some that Sergei Korolev, V.P. Glushko, and Artem Mikoyan (of MiG fighter fame) had an early involvement with Soviet space shuttle conceptualization.[27] For many years it was speculated that this space shuttle would be much smaller than the current American space shuttle, perhaps being similar in concept to the proposed USAF/Boeing X-20 'Dyna-Soar'. Developed in the United States during the 1960s as a follow-on to the X-15 series, Dyna-Soar never left the prototype stage before being cancelled. It would have involved a relatively small-winged space-plane launched on top of an expendable booster such as a Titan 3. ESA's 'Hermes' space-plane planned for the 1990s is also to employ this concept.

It was believed that the Soviet 'Raketoplan' (rocket aircraft)[28] was to be a lifting body configuration that could be launched either on top of a conventional booster, such as Proton, or from an advanced re-usable hypersonic 'flyback' booster.[29] Drop-tests of prototype vehicles from Tupolev Tu-95 Bear bombers may have occurred as early as 1975.[30] While up to the early 1980s some Soviet officials and scientists made vague statements concerning the development of a re-usable space shuttle capability, no official confirmation was provided to the west.

A clear indication of Soviet activity in this area did not occur until the testing on 3 June 1982 of a sub-scale, unmanned prototype winged spacecraft designated Cosmos 1374.[31] The test lasted only one and a half orbits at NEO before ending with a successful re-entry over the Indian Ocean and a parachute landing and recovery near the Cocos Islands, some 2,300 km north-west of Australia. This test had followed an announcement by Soviet officials that the development of a shuttle-type winged re-usable manned spacecraft would be an integral part of their advanced space station activities.[32] The second mission (Cosmos 1445) also involved an Indian Ocean recovery, but the subsequent third and fourth missions ended with recoveries in the Black Sea.[33]

The exact intent of these four flight tests has been the subject of some debate. Each of the 1,000 kg vehicles was launched from Kapustin Yar, a Cosmodrome not associated with manned spaceflight, on a small expendable booster. Some analysts believe a similarity exists between these tests and the USAF 'Prime' and 'Asset' programmes of the 1960s in which aerothermodynamic and aerothermo-elastic structural systems environmental test gliders were launched on sub-orbital flights on Thor and Atlas boosters from Cape Canaveral. Photographs of the Soviet space-planes' recoveries in the Indian Ocean indicate a combination lifting body/delta-wing design with twin vertical stabilizers similar to the USAF X-24B experimental glider. One hypothesis is that the Soviet test vehicles were sub-scale versions of an operational 18,000-kg-class manned space-plane. To this extent distinct windshield, crew cabin design, and thermal tile protection features were apparent on the test vehicles. The operational space-plane would be launched on the new MLV from Tyuratam; eventually it could be mated with a fly-back booster. NASA's Langley Research Centre has completed a series of wind-tunnel analyses on models of the Soviet prototype space-plane which indicate that it flies its re-entry embedded within its own bow shock wave.[34] This characteristic is important because it indicates that the space-plane would have lower overall re-entry heating temperatures than larger space shuttle designs that have wings protruding outside the shock wave. A corresponding requirement for less stringent thermal protection could allow the use of less complicated re-usable heatshields, compared to the complex system of protective thermal tiles employed on American space shuttles.

96

However, some critics are sceptical about the space-plane's actually being scaled to a larger manned vehicle because the Soviets routinely test large numbers of aircraft prototypes that are not put into actual production. Alternatively the space-plane could be a technology demonstrator for a heavy space shuttle design, or even an orbital, cross-range manoeuvrable anti-ship nuclear weapon.[35] In support of the latter theory, the prototype vehicles exhibited excellent cross-range flights of over 600 kilometres. Given the Soviet propensity for applying proven designs to various problems, the space plane programme could indeed have multiple applications in all of these areas!

If the Soviet space-plane does mature into an operational vehicle it could have various interesting operational capabilities. It would offer only minimal crew size (perhaps three cosmonauts) and pay-load advantages over the current Soyuz TM spacecraft. It would be completely re-usable and could provide light logistics support for manned space stations and satellite repair and maintenance (a role similar to that planned for ESA's Hermes). Direct military applications are a possibility.[36] The space-plane could conceivably be equipped with both chemical and electric rocket propulsion systems for orbital manoeuvres. Speculation that the Soviet space-plane could also be equipped with jet engines to permit powered aerodynamic manoeuvring and landings is doubtful given the vehicle's small projected size, but should not be entirely discounted. The space-plane will likely not be restricted to a single orbital inclination for each mission, as is the American space shuttle, but could have a flexible multiple orbit-to-orbit capability. This could be accomplished through the vehicle's basic design allowing it to employ 'aero-capture' techniques in which it would initiate re-entry procedures, dip into the atmosphere, aerodynamically provide course changes with small fuel consumption penalties, and then use its on-board propulsion system to re-inject into a new orbit. This operation could be repeated several times per mission in quick succession.

Such a high manoeuvrability capability would be instrumental in defining many of the space-plane's specific military missions which could include:

1 A weapons platform for directed-energy, kinetic projectiles, EW, and nuclear weapons.
2 Satellite inspection and destruction, with a limited BMD role.
3 A strike-bomber role against high-priority terrestrial targets, thereby combining the great speeds of ICBMs and the

'␣re-callability' of manned bombers (an original mission for the X-20 Dyna-Soar).

4 A C^3I function, including 'stealth' reconnaissance flights over enemy territory at altitudes too high for conventional aircraft and too low for satellites.

5 A general utility role that would include the provision of security for military and commercial space facilities, the repair and maintenance of satellites and man-tended platforms, and a 'rescue vehicle' function for stranded cosmonauts or astronauts.

If these somewhat speculative capabilities did indeed materialize, the vehicle could be considered the world's first *space-fighter*. This would prove to be very ironic given the repeated Soviet charges claiming the American space shuttle to be an offensive weapon system.[37]

By 1983 the United States Defense Department publicly revealed that the Soviet Union was also developing a large space shuttle comparable in design and dimensions to NASA's own.[38] Initial reports indicated a projected relatively low total lift-off weight combined with a high thrust. This combination could result in a pay-load capability to NEO almost double that of the American space shuttle. However, subsequent estimates of the Soviet shuttle's projected pay-load capability have been revised downwards to approximately that of the American capability (30,000 kg).[39] Extensive support facilities for the space shuttle and HLV programme have been observed under development at the Tyuratam Cosmodrome which include a space shuttle landing strip, large new launch pads and vehicle assembly buildings, and cryogenic fuel storage facilities. Atmospheric tests of large shuttle vehicles were centred around the Ramenskoye flight test centre just east of Moscow. By 1984 initial approach and landing drop tests were conducted from modified Myasishchev Mya-4 Bison bomber carrier aircraft.[40] During 1986 the programme evidently progressed to include the addition of jet engines to the space shuttle to provide more flexible approach and landing capabilities.[41] It is believed possible that the Soviet space shuttle may now also be capable of taking off under the power of its integral jet engines for training purposes. Such advanced developments appears to be indicative of a programme rapidly maturing in the areas of flight control systems, computers, and software, auxiliary power units, and simulation capabilities. Recent developments have included the integration of the shuttle orbiter to the HLV booster.

The design, and even the mere existence, of the Soviet heavy space shuttle has been quite controversial in the west. Unlike the American system, the Soviet orbiter has no integral main engines, but rather will be mounted on the Energia HLV. Solid propellant boosters are not used. A likely operational configuration will be similar to that employed for Energia's maiden flight: four liquid fuel strap-on boosters and a heavy space shuttle substituting for an unmanned pay-load pod. This configuration will allow the Soviet space shuttle to have greater potential pay-loads and the use of integral jet engines for limited atmospheric manoeuvring (fuel loads will be minimal). It is likely that the Soviets will restrict the use of their space shuttle to sensitive missions that require a manned presence (for example, the construction of large structures or the deployment of delicate systems), and employ the Energia and other unmanned boosters to perform the bulk of pay-load delivery to orbit. This contrasts sharply with the past American approach which had emphasized an over-reliance on their space shuttle transportation system, and resulted in a serious launch capability degradation after the Challenger accident. The Americans, following the Soviet example, are now undertaking a launch recovery programme that will emphasize the use of unmanned launch vehicles for routine tasks.

It has been charged that the basic configuration of the Soviet heavy space shuttle is very close to that of the American orbiter, and that this is a direct result of the Soviet acquisition, by legal means, of NASA technical specifications and documentation, and American computers and advanced machinery.[42] However, while the Soviets have likely profited from western technology transfer for this project, superficial design similarities may also be a result of optimum configuration requirements (the proposed European Hermes space-plane also resembles the American design to a certain extent). While the Soviet orbiter may resemble the American space shuttle, its overall system design, as noted previously, is quite different.

Some sceptics have downplayed both the Soviet space-plane and heavy space shuttle programmes as being colossal 'red herrings' on various grounds: the reports have been the results of a combination of exaggerated American fears and Soviet misinformation; the Soviets lack the technical sophistication to develop such complex systems in the near term; or the development of such reusable vehicles would be contrary to current or foreseeable Soviet space transportation needs.[43] In addition, until recently Soviet cosmonauts, scientists, and officials often provided contradictory statements to the west which downplayed the necessity and desirability of space shuttle systems.[44] However, after the successful demonstration of their technological prowess with Energia, the Soviets have officially admitted the existence of their programme and their intention to use space shuttle vehicles to support space station and various other operations.[45] Soviet space shuttle and space-plane activities are now very likely to begin in earnest by the late 1980s, perhaps proceeding to supersede the initial American advantage in this area.

MANNED SPACE STATIONS

The second generation Salyut ('space station') 6 and 7 manned space stations resulted in the evolutionary improvement of Soviet manned space operations during the 1970s and early 1980s.[46] These steady improvements are providing the building blocks for more advanced space station projects.

Incremental technical improvements to Salyut 6 included a second docking port at the end of the station's longitudinal axis which permitted the simultaneous berthing of the resident crew's Soyuz transport, and either another visiting crew's Soyuz or a Prognoz supply vehicle. The station refuelling process was refined by the incorporation of pressure-fed engines and thrusters. Although crew living quarters remained rather cramped, amenities such as a shower and permanent water recycling facilities were added.

Salyut 6 activities included extensive internal repairs by Cosmonauts Leonid Kizim, Oleg Makarov, and Gennadiy Strekalov to extend the station's life during December 1980,[47] and by Cosmonauts Vladimir Kovalenok and Viktor Savinykh during March 1981.[48]

An emphasis was placed during Salyut 6 operations on the continued extended duration of human spaceflight in possible preparation for interplanetary voyages, and the manufacturing of space-processed products, such as semi-conductor materials, as a near-term commercial activity. A significant event was the demonstration of the modular assembly of large space station elements by linking Cosmos 1267 with Salyut 6 on 19 June 1981.[49] Cosmos 1267 initially had displayed characteristics very similar to those of the November 1978 Cosmos 929, which was believed by some analysts to represent a major test of a manned-spaceflight-oriented system. Cosmos 929 manoeuvred extensively before returning a large re-entry vehicle to earth, an activity that was duplicated by Cosmos 1267 before it joined Salyut 6. The pronounced delta-v (acceleration) of these vehicles was indicative of a possible space-tug role. Docking the 13,600 kg Cosmos 1267 to the 19,000 kg Salyut 6 practically doubled the space station's size and increased its overall length to 30 metres. The module was characterized by the Soviets as a building block leading towards the development of future permanently manned modular space stations which would include astronomical observatories, microgravity manufacturing plants, and crew habitats. Such modular elements would be attached to a central core equipped with multiple docking ports. Towards this end, the 1267 class vehicle is an extension of Salyut level technology. The re-entry module could be used for the return of space-manufactured products such as semi-conductor materials and pharmaceuticals. In addition, there were unconfirmed charges from the United States that Cosmos 1267 was a 'space battleship' equipped with infra-red-homing missiles. It remained docked to Salyut 6 for over a year of unmanned engineering tests. After a four-year, ten-month mission that included 676 days of manned operations spread over five long-duration crews, Salyut 6 and Cosmos 1267 were commanded into a destructive re-entry over the Pacific Ocean on 29 July 1982.

Salyut 7 was launched on 19 April 1982, in the midst of much speculation that it might incorporate significant improvements such as a third docking port for greater flexibility and expansion with the use of Cosmos 1267 class modules.[50] In fact, Salyut 7 was virtually identical to its predcecessor. Its main technical improvements consisted of incremental modifications such as superior docking structures, computers, and crew facilities. On 14 May 1982 Cosmonauts Anatoliy Berezovoy and Valentin Lebedev were transported to the space station as the long-duration crew. They were closely followed by a guest crew consisting of Cosmonauts Vladimir Djanibekov and Alexander Ivanchenkov, along with the French mission specialist Jean-Loup Chretien. Significant Salyut 7 crew activities included:

1 A 237-day record sojourn by Cosmonauts Leonid Kizim, Vladimir Solovyev, and Oleg Atkov from 8 February 1984 to 2 October 1984, which included extensive EVAs to repair a crippled propulsion system and augment the station's power supply by erecting supplementary solar panels.[51]

2 EVAs by Cosmonauts Lebedev and Berezovoy on 30 July 1982, related to the assembly of future large-scale space structures.[52]

3 The Soyuz T-13 mission by Cosmonauts Vladimir Djanibekov and Viktor Savinykh on 6 June 1985 to repair and reactivate the space station after an almost total electrical power failure.[53]

4 Further EVAs by Cosmonauts Kizim and Solovyev during a

late May 1986 mission to demonstrate the construction of large space structures, including a 15-metre aluminium pylon.[54]

Another significant development was the 2 March 1983 launch of Cosmos 1443 which, having characteristics similar to Cosmos 1267, was finally confirmed by the Soviets as being a space station tug and electrical power module that can transport heavy cargo to and from large space facilities.[55] Equipped with a Gemini-sized re-entry vehicle, the Cosmos-Zvezda ('Star') multi-purpose space tug and expansion module was revealed to have the following characteristics:

1 A re-entry vehicle capable of returning 500 kg of cargo (such as research materials and bulk microgravity produced products) to earth.
2 About 40 square metres of solar arrays capable of generating some 3 kW of electrical power to support such operations as materials processing.
3 A heavy propellant load to provide a significant increase in space station manoeuvrability (fuel can also be transferred to and from the tug and space station).
4 A heavy re-supply capability of about 3 tonnes of cargo (over twice the capability of a Prognoz resupply vehicle).
5 The capability for space station modular expansion (50 cubic metres of work area), and specialized modules for applications such as astrophysics, materials processing, and military missions.
6 The capability to detach itself into a free-flyer configuration to provide a very stable microgravity environment for experimentation and manufacturing processes.

On 27 September 1985 a second Star space-tug, Cosmos 1686, was launched to Salyut 7, evidently replacing Cosmos 1443.[56] Currently the Soviets appear prepared to keep Salyut 7 in readiness during the nest several years for possible manned operations in conjunction with the Mir space station.[57] Another possible role for Salyut 7 is that of a system-longevity test for degradation assessments for such future activities as a manned Mars expedition.

In a surprise move, the Soviets launched a third-generation space station called Mir ('Peace') on 20 February 1986.[58] (The new name was undoubtedly selected to emphasize Soviet opposition to SDI!) Superficially Mir is a clear evolutionary development of its Salyut predecessors. To a certain extent this configuration similarity was determined by the use of a common launch vehicle, the Proton. A primary improvement are Mir's six docking ports, compared with only two on Salyuts 6 and 7. While the previous Salyuts had a docking port at each end of the cylindrical space station structure, Mir has an additional four ports spaced at ninety-degree intervals around its circumference at the forward-end transfer compartment. These are to be mated with specialized modules, some likely derived from the Star-class vehicle, for long durations. This will result in a considerable growth in the size of the space station at angles perpendicular to the main space station body, unlike the earlier Salyuts which could be expanded only along one axis. Specialized functions of the modules will include astrophysical research, biological/pharmaceutical, and other materials production. The modules will employ manipulator devices to transfer from the main docking port to one of the lateral ports. The 13.13-metre-long body of the space station is to be primarily devoted to the crew's habitation, complete with individual crew cabins and a large galley. Crew size will be either five or six. An enlarged set of three solar panels (possibly employing advanced gallium arsenide rather than silicon cells) provides over 10 kW of electric power, more than twice that of the Salyuts. Electronics and computer systems have also been significantly increased. A major improvement in space-to-ground communications has been accomlished via the Luch (Beam) relay satellite, for applications such as remote station control, diagnostics, and data transmission. Mir's command centre is equipped with separate visual screens for each of the eight computers which control all on-board systems.

Given the current Proton launch rate, the current 21-tonne Mir space station could be expanded to a 120-tonne, six-module structure by 1992 to 1994. Initially some observers felt a Mir-Salyut 7 link-up to be imminent; however this has not materialized to date. It is likely that they will keep these stations separate. Cosmonauts Leonid Kizim and Vladimir Solovyev arrived at Mir aboard Soyuz T-15 on 15 March 1986. After spending seven weeks aboard Mir for systems check-outs, they travelled to Salyut 7 in the first station-to-station transfer on 5–6 May 1986.[59] Such orbital transfers are an important step towards their stated intention of creating 'Oblakos', or swarms of orbital laboratories and space stations. Kizim and Solovyev returned to Mir on 26 June 1986, and to Earth on 16 July 1986 after spending 125 days in space. Mir continued to be serviced by robotic Prognoz transport spacecraft with Prognoz 27 docking with the space station on 18 January 1987.

On 6 February 1987 the second Mir crew consisting of Cosmonauts

Yuri Romanenko and Alexander Laveikin was launched on Soyuz TM-2.[60] The Soyuz TM-2 spacecraft was the first operational use of this improved design that was first tested in an unmanned flight and Mir link-up of May 1986. The current crew mission is of long duration and will emphasize crew EVAs and space station expansion with new modules. The ultimate goal is the establishment of a permanently manned facility, which the Soviets are rapidly reaching. The United States will not be able to match this capability until the mid-1990s at the earliest.

After some initial docking difficulties, the Kvant ('Quantum') astrophysics module was linked, with the crew's extra-vehicular assistance, to Mir's stern on 12 April 1987.[61] This addition increased Mir's length some 50 per cent. Kvant incorporates advanced equipment supplied by the Soviet Union, the Netherlands, Britain, ESA, and West Germany, and will add to the growing Soviet space science capability.

On 30 July 1987 Cosmonaut Laveikin, who developed suspected heart problems, exchanged his post with Cosmonaut Alexander Alexandrov of the visiting three-man Soyuz TM-3 crew. Materials processing and Earth resources photographic modules will probably expand the Mir space station throughout 1987 and 1988.

Several growing trends have characterized Soviet space station development. Most apparent is the dual military applications discussed in Chapter 3. Military applications have ranged from surveillance, laser pointing and tracking tests, and support for combined arms military exercises and tests. Such manned capabilities could be an important element of future Soviet BMD, ASAT, and other military space systems. The Soviets have developed impressive space station remote-sensing and materials-processing capabilities and are now more eager to market these services internationally. Increasingly bolder and innovative techniques for space station operations and expansion are being employed. EVAs are becoming routine. An emphasis is being placed on international co-operation. Western nations, in particular France, are becoming more receptive to participating with Soviet space station projects. France has recently opened discussions with the Soviet Union to ensure that the Hermes space-plane will be able to dock with Mir and other Soviet space stations during the 1990s.[62] A French 'spacionaute', Jean Loup Chretien, is to have a Mir mission in 1988, following similar past participation with Salyut 7. Other space station guest astronauts will come from Syria and Bulgaria, while offers of participation have also been extended to Britain and Canada.

The Soviets have various options for their future space station developments at a time when similar American efforts have been seriously delayed and hindered. The basic infrastructure has been developed to support large-scale modular space station developments: Salyut/Mir base modules; Star space-tug/expansion modules; Kvant-type expansion modules; Prognoz robotic supply/tanker spacecraft; and steadily upgraded Soyuz crew-ferrying spacecraft. These systems are being produced on an assembly-line basis and are becoming steadily more reliable. Numerous Mirs and expansion modules could be linked in parallel to form large manned complexes. However, newly emerging systems will steadily complement and eventually supersede these proven capabilities. The Energia HLV and heavy space shuttle will be capable of delivering core modules much larger than Mir. The small space-plane could be used for crew ferrying and light re-supply. The new MLV could eventually replace Proton for space station support missions. Nuclear reactors could be used to provide much greater, and more compact, power supplies than are readily availble from solar cells: given their past record with RORSAT, the Soviets are much more likely than the west to adopt such systems for manned applications. A recent Soviet interest has also been expressed in large-scale solar power satellite system (SPSS) development, which would be closely tied to a massive manned space operations capability. A greater Soviet emphasis will have to be placed on the operational introduction of close-looped environmental control systems in order to support the 100-plus cosmonaut space stations that could be deployed by the turn-of-the-century. (Salyut and Mir are essentially open-loop systems in that all food supplies, and most air requirements, are dependent upon ground support and replenishment). Such close-looped systems would also be supportive of manned interplanetary expeditions. Large manned space operations centres will provide the orbital construction bases and control centres for future Soviet military, commercial, scientific, and exploratory initiatives. Such activities could specifically include a staging area for manned flights to the Moon and Mars, and a laboratory and quarantine area for returning missions that could possibly harbour extra-terrestrial contaminants. Towards this visionary goal, the Soviets have recently solicited international co-operation for the proposed development of a fourth-generation 'Mir 2' space station, the assembly of which is to begin after 1992.[63] This is to comprise a 100-tonne core vehicle launched by the Energia HLV, and 20-tonne expansion modules delivered by Proton launchers.

7

Scientific and interplanetary exploration

OVERVIEW

During the past decade there has been an aggressive growth in Soviet interplanetary exploration and general space science. Paralleling this has been an apparent American shift away from space science after initiating a successful wide-sweeping reconnaissance of the Solar System during the 1960s and 1970s. Increasing European and Japanese activities in these areas has stimulated their interest in active participation with planned Soviet missions. Significant international co-operation has already been provided for the successful Soviet Vega mission to Venus and Halley's Comet.

There is an overall continuity to Soviet planetary exploration. During the 1960s numerous missions concentrated on the Moon. The 1970s and early 1980s saw an effort concentrated on Venus. Into the 1990s the focus of Soviet planetary exploration is shifting to Mars and minor bodies such as the martian moons, asteroids, and comets. Current Soviet commitments for planetary exploration during the next decade will eclipse those proposed by the west, many of which are still at a conceptual stage. Significant Soviet efforts will be underway for the International Space Year in 1992, which is to be comparable to the 1957 Geophysical Year (the year in which Sputnik 1 was launched).

The Soviets are currently placing a great emphasis on developing co-operative scientific space activities with the west. Soviet motives for such increased co-operation are a straightforward desire to improve their own scientific capabilities through the acquisition of advanced western technologies, decrease expensive programme costs, and the avoidance of duplicative efforts. There is, in addition, a true element of co-operative goodwill, with corresponding international political

106

benefits. Space co-operation with the Soviet Union is often viewed by the United States as a means of reducing political tensions, and possibly providing sufficient leverage to induce desirable Soviet political change.[1] Such co-operation also provides an opportunity to learn more about Soviet society and to provide an open window of communications. However, to date western co-operation with Soviet space projects has had no discernible effect upon either their foreign or domestic policies — whether this would also be true for a major effort such as a US/Soviet manned mission to Mars remains open to question. The Americans also have grave concerns regarding the transfer of sensitive, military-applicable technologies to the Soviets through co-operative space ventures.

Soviet/US space co-operation suffered during most of the 1980s as a result of aggressive Soviet actions in Afghanistan and Poland, but was tentatively rejuvenated in 1987 with the ratification of a new space co-operative agreement.[2] This step was highly significant given the consistent Soviet opposition towards SDI as being a stumbling block for joint space efforts. In general, this new agreement centres on programmes which will co-ordinate separate projects, and the exchange of data rather than the joint development of mission hardware. Examples of such planned co-operative activities include:

1   The co-ordinated study of Soviet Venera 15 and 16 Venus radar data in conjunction with the planning and operation of the American Magellan Venus radar mapper set for launch in 1989.
2   The use of the US Deep Space Tracking Network to receive signals from Soviet exploratory spacecraft.
3   A more detailed and co-ordinated exchange of data from US/Soviet astronomical and astrophysics missions.
4   New life sciences data exchanges of cosmonaut medical records from Salyut/Mir missions and astronaut data from American space shuttle flights.
5   The use of simple US hardware on Soviet bio-satellites carrying research animals, and the joint analysis of data from such flights.

Data exchanges between the planned Soviet Mars/Phobos and Mars/Vesta missions and the tentative American Mars Observer mission could open the way for a more substantive collaboration. This could include a joint Mars Sample Return mission to return Martian rock and soil samples to Earth, or even a joint manned mission to Mars after the turn-of-the-century. Needless to say, such collaborative efforts will be discouraged by American technology transfer and prestige concerns. It now appears likely that the Soviets will eventually attempt manned Mars missions with or without American participation.

Given the American reluctance to support Soviet exploratory efforts directly through technological hardware contributions, the Soviets will increasingly turn to western Europe, Japan, and even Canada for such support (notwithstanding the COCAM agreement that restricts the sale of sensitive technologies to Communist nations). France has had bilateral co-operative agreements with the Soviet Union for over a decade, and these appear to be largely immune to ongoing political events. In 1986 Britain and the Soviet Union entered into a ten-year agreement to co-operate in various areas of space science, including the development, construction, and launching of actual hardware.[3] Canada's National Research Council is currently developing an ultraviolet imager for a Soviet magnetospheric research satellite,[4] and both countries have recently discussed collaborative efforts in such areas as space telescopes, manned space stations, and manned missions to Mars. These co-operative activities are occurring during the implementation of a *glasnost* approach to the Soviet space programme in which details of its scientific and commercial activities are becoming more familiar in the west. Current indications are that this co-operative trend will be long term in nature.

VENUS PROGRAMME

A total of nineteen Soviet probes have been sent to Venus during the past twenty-five years. The twin Vega spacecraft represented the culmination of the most recent Venus exploration series, which began in 1975 with Veneras 9 and 10. Pairs of probes were sent to Venus every few years and employed the conservative strategy of using the same basic spacecraft design, while incrementally upgrading scientific instrumentation for each mission. Although encountering some difficulties (most notably Veneras 11 and 12 which reached the planet's surface but transmitted no data) the Venus programme maintained a steady pace. Highlights of this programme included the first black and white photographs of another planet sent by the Venera 9 and 10 landers; soil and colour photographic analyses conducted by Veneras 13 and 14; and the first imaging radar maps of the Venusian surface produced by Veneras 15 and 16.[5] These accomplishments were even more significant given the extremely hostile Venusian environment of immense atmospheric pressures, corrosive gases, and 400°C surface temperatures!

Although the United States had provided limited co-operation with earlier Venera missions, Vegas 1 and 2 were notable for the intense international participation and media coverage that was generated by a Soviet space mission.[6] This mission involved the twin spacecraft swinging around Venus and dropping a pair of French-developed weather balloons into the planet's upper atmosphere on the way to a Halley's Comet fly-by. In addition, descent probes similar to those used on previous missions were deployed on the Venusian surface. The balloons arrived on 11 and 15 June 1985 and drifted amongst the Venusian cloud tops for over a day, communicating a detailed profile of the planet's high-altitude temperatures, pressures, and wind dynamics. The Vega balloons, in essence, made the first in-situ observations of 'weather' on another world. For example, as the Vega 2 balloon passed some 50 kilometres above Aphrodite, one of the highest mountains on Venus, it encountered *vertical* winds of up to 11 kilometres per hour.

The technical challenge of the Vega mission was a primary reason for the wide Soviet invitation for international participation. It now appears that the amount of data obtained from this and previous missions will satisfy the Soviet curiosity about Venus for some time, as no further missions are currently planned.

COMET AND ASTEROID EXPLORATION

The Vega cometary mission appears to be the first of the new wave of ambitious Soviet planetary exploration missions. The twin Vega spacecraft used in the fly-by of Halley's Comet carried experimental pay-loads and instrumentation developed in co-operation with France, West Germany, Austria, Czechoslovakia, Hungary, Bulgaria and Poland. American researchers participated in Vega data analysis.

The Soviet cometary encounter was one of several international missions to study Halley's Comet in 1986. Other missions were made by ESA (Giotto) and Japan. The potentially superior US Halley Intercept Mission did not materialize owing to a lack of political support and resulting NASA budgetary constraints and conflicting programme priorities. However, NASA, ESA, and Intercosmos co-operated for the navigation communications requirements of the various Halley missions.

The Vega cometary probe three-axis-stabilized spacecraft were derived from the spacecraft bus design that was used to deliver landers during previous Venus missions. However, the Vega spacecraft were equipped with very specialized, advanced instrumentation such as spectrometers (three channel, infra-red, dust mass, neutral gas mass, and ion mass), dust particle encounters, electron analysers, high-energy particle counters, plasma wave analysers, magnetometers, and digital television imagers. Pay-loads for each spacecraft totalled 120 kg.

Vega made its closest encounter with Halley's Comet at a distance of 8,480 kilometres on 6 March 1986, and Vega 2 at 8,000 kilometres on 9 March 1986. ESA's Giotto came to within 500 kilometres range on 13 March 1986, while the two Japanese probes provided only long-distance observations. The Soviet probes provided the first view of the hypothesized cometary ice and rock core through high-resolution false colour images. A broad base of data was successfully provided on cometary physical composition, dust conditions, infra-red radiation, magnetic fields, plasmas, and other characteristics of the cometary environment.

Some consideration has been made to re-target Vega 2 for a fly-by of the asteroid Adonis in 1987, but apparently this step was not taken.[7] The estimated power reduction to Vega 2 attributed to dust particle impacts during the cometary fly-by was some 50 per cent, and this could prohibit future exploratory activities. However, Vega 1 also appears to be available for re-targeted missions. Such a mission could provide another Soviet space first: close-up photographs and sensor analysis of an asteroid.

The Soviet Union is now completing the design of a new unmanned spacecraft for future planetary and lunar missions as a follow-on to the proven Venera design.[8] This new configuration could be employed for the planned 'Vesta' Mars/comet/asteroid fly-by mission (which was originally targeted at Venus). A co-operative venture with France, the mid-1990s Vesta mission is expected to provide data on at least five different asteroids and comets during a five-year flight period. The mission also represents the first attempt at exploring the potentially resource-rich 'asteroid belt' between Mars and Jupiter. Twin spacecraft will be launched on a Mars trajectory by 1994, and each will include a Mars orbiter and possibly re-entry probes. The secondary vehicle component of each main spacecraft will be a French-designed asteroid/comet fly-by vehicle. Penetrators may be fired from these to asteroid surfaces for composition analyses. It is also possible that actual asteroid samples could be returned to Earth. Design improvements for the new generation of modular interplanetary spacecraft that the Soviets are planning to use for the Vesta and other future missions will include:[9]

1 A multi-task liquid fuel propulsion system optimized for specific missions to Mars, Venus, the Moon, and other Solar System bodies.
2 A separate propulsion system, integral to the spacecraft, for braking and correction manoeuvres.
3 The capability to adapt the spacecraft for landings on planetary bodies by the use of extendable supports.
4 A modular design of the spacecraft's upper section to allow the integration of mission-specific instrumentation and pay-loads.

MARS PROGRAMME

The major focus of future Soviet interplanetary research and exploration will once more be Mars. These planned activities, unmanned probes, and likely manned missions, will end the Soviet Mars mission hiatus extending back to 1973. In contrast to the full agenda planned by the Soviets, the only similar American commitmment is the solitary Mars Observer to be launched in 1992, which is intended to map the planet from low orbit.

Numerous factors have been cited as justification for the human exploration and eventual colonization of Mars:[10]

1 It is the most agreeable planet for extraterrestrial human habitation in the Solar System, given the presence of suitable amounts of water and various other resource materials necessary for the production of air, food, fuels, fertilizers, and building materials.
2 Mars holds a strategic position within the Solar System — in effect the 'gateway' to the resource-rich outer planets and asteroid belt.
3 The planet is a possible home of native life, and is interesting from various other research perspectives such as geological and climatic change.
4 Martian exploration is almost a natural focus for an adventuresome, prestigious, possibly internationally co-operative, space programme — Mars has fascinated the human race throughout history.

The boldness and complexity of Soviet Martian exploration plans have recently startled the western scientific community.[11] However, since the early days of the Soviet space programme there appears to have been an underlying objective of the exploration of Mars and the entire Solar System. The new Soviet programme will commence with the Phobos mission launch of twin spacecraft in 1988.[12] The objective of this innovative mission is the close analysis of Mars and one of its moons, Phobos. It will also be the first spacecraft rendezvous/landing with a small Solar System body. The other Martian moon, Demos, could also be targeted if the first spacecraft is successful. In each case, the main spacecraft will study Martian geology, atmospherics, and climate from orbit, in addition to depositing two small landers on a moon's surface. The Phobos main spacecraft will manoeuvre to orbit in hover formation within 50 metres of the Martian moon's surface, and will fire both laser and ion particle beams to vapourize surface material for analysis. One deposited lander will consist of a long-term experimental package to study soil chemistry and orbital variations. A second lander will comprise a short-term 'hopper' vehicle that will literally jump from location to location to provide extensive surface condition information. The mission is to emphasize international co-operation and will include instrumentation and experiments from Bulgaria, West Germany, Britain, Sweden, France, and Austria. NASA will provide assistance through the use of its deep-space-tracking network to receive communications signals from the Soviet spacecraft.[13] The Phobos mission is extremely important in terms of future *manned* Martian missions because it should indicate the moon's potential use as a source of relatively inexpensive water and fuel sources.[14]

The next step of the Soviet Mars programme is to be a very large satellite sent there by 1992–4 which will carry two surface penetrators, balloons, and possibly a small (200–250 kg) wheeled rover vehicle.[15] The balloons will drift over vast distances of the Martian surface during the day, land during the cool nights to collect samples, and take off again during the day when the atmosphere warms up. The 1992 mission could be followed by a 1994–6 spacecraft(s) equipped to land large, long-range rovers and robotic 'moles' that could tunnel under the Martian surface in search of water and life. By 1996–8 an unmanned sample-return mission could be conducted, possibly in co-operation with the United States. The sum total of projected Soviet pay-loads sent to Mars from 1988 to 1996 will be at least 45,000 kg. By the turn-of-the-century robotic rovers could have provided the necessary reconnaissance for a manned mission. It is interesting to note that an underlying motivation to these Soviet exploration plans is a fundamental rejection of the American Viking probes' conclusions that native life does not exist on Mars.[16]

The sum total of the Soviet Mars reconnaissance programme combined with their other maturing spaceflight capabilities points to a manned mission to Mars by the year 2000. The current and emerging capabilities relevant to a Soviet manned mission to Mars are:

1 A permanently manned space station for the construction of large structures at NEO (Mars mission ships will be large and will likely have to be assembled in orbit).
2 Long-duration manned missions such as those conducted on the Salyut/Mir space stations which have demonstrated successful human endurance in a weightless, radiation-intense environment for long periods of time (given current propulsion technology restraints, a round-trip Mars mission will likely be at least two and a half years in total).
3 The development of close-looped environmental support systems and long-endurance space hardware.
4 Hardware developments such as the Energia HLV, space tugs, nuclear propulsion systems and past experience in landing vehicles gained during the old Soviet Moon programme with such vehicles as Zond and likely analogues to the Apollo lander.

The Mars mission could take the form of an actual manned landing, fly-by, observation from orbit, or a landing on one of the moons. To date the Soviets have not announced their specific intentions, possibly to avoid another 'Moon Race' with the United States. An international Mars unmanned sample-return and/or manned mission has been widely touted as being politically and scientifically desirable, and the Soviets appear to be open to such collaboration with the west. However, it should be considered that an underlying mandate of NASA is to attempt to maintain clear American space leadership. Technology transfer and military implications aside, it is doubtful that the United States would be anxious to co-operate as an equal partner with the Soviet Union for reasons of national pride alone. However, as the Soviet Mars programme rapidly unfolds it is providing the direct threat of relegating the United States to second-class space power status. The effects of this far-reaching programme will also provide synergistic improvements to Soviet military space capabilities that are difficult to predict at this time.

OTHER SCIENTIFIC ACTIVITIES

After ending their lunar exploration programme in 1976, the Soviets are now planning a return to the Moon in the form of a lunar polar orbiter mission for the early 1990s.[17] This mission is to expand the knowledge base of the Moon's chemical and mineral composition, magnetic fields and temperatures. This activity is targeted for 1991 and will involve a large unmanned satellite in a lunar north-south polar orbit that will for the first time provide geochemical mapping of the entire lunar surface. Analysis is to concentrate on the still largely unknown lunar dark side and polar regions. The Soviets are also co-operating with the Americans in the selection of potential lunar landing sites for manned or unmanned missions.[18] Such activity could signal the impending resumption of Soviet manned lunar exploration efforts. Although not a scientific prerequisite, a manned lunar base would be a logical operational precursor to a manned Mars mission. Such missions are well within the capabilities of the new Energia HLV, and it is possible that a Soviet manned lunar base could be established by the turn-of-the-century.

Various future space science missions, many in connection with the 1992 International Space Year, are currently being planned by the Soviets:[19]

1. 'Project Medilab' — a dedicated medical laboratory docked to the Mir space station by the early 1990s for advanced animal and human medical microgravity research.
2. 'Project Priroda' — a large Mir module for international remote sensing projects.
3. 'Project Bion' — expanded international co-operation for the ongoing biological satellite programme which has conducted numerous missions with animals in recoverable spacecraft based upon the early Vostok design.
4. 'Relikt-2' spacecraft — an unusual 1991–3 mission that will see the placing of a Soviet spacecraft at a strategic Lagrangian libration point to conduct a sky survey of galactic background information.
5. 'Gamma 1' spacecraft — a 1988 7-tonne Soviet/French space-based gamma-ray telescope.
6. 'Granat' spacecraft — a 1988 Soviet/French high-energy astrophysics mission.
7. 'Radio Astron' spacecraft — an early 1990s 10-metre radio astronomy telescope. This mission will evolve into a series

of satellite radio telescopes equipped with large antennas for VLBI (very long baseline interferometry) measurements in co-ordination with ground-based radio telescopes.

8   'Aelita' observatory spacecraft — a 1992–5 7-tonne spacecraft carrying a sub-millimetre actively cooled telescope for the observation of extremely low-temperature objects in deep space.

9   'Spectral-Roentgen' spacecraft — a 1992–4 specialized mission for extreme ultra-violet observations of deep space.

10   Space plasma missions — at least three Soviet space plasma projects will include the 1988 'Aktivnyi' satellite for magnetospheric observation; the 1989 'Apeks' spacecraft; and the 'Interbol' mission set for 1990 which will launch two satellites for co-operative space plasma science opportunities.

11   'Project Corona' — a 1995 launch for a fly-by of the Sun to within five to seven radii.

12   Outer planet exploration — By 1999 various spacecraft could be sent to Jupiter and Saturn, including one which is to explore the atmosphere and surface of the Saturnian moon Titan.

In addition to these proposed far-sweeping missions (which may not all have final budgetary approval), the Soviets have maintained an active programme for the search/communication of extraterrestrial intelligence (CETI).[20] Under the auspices of the Soviet Academy of Sciences, the current emphasis in this field appears to be on the detection, through the use of optical and infra-red/laser detection devices, of vast astro-engineering structures in space developed by alien 'super-civilizations'. While there was a great deal of Soviet activity during the 1960s and 1970s for the detection of extraterrestrial radio emissions with radio telescopes, such activity has recently declined. However, given the current rapid development pace of Soviet space science, the use of space-based radio telescopes and other devices for Soviet CETI purposes is a distinct possibility.

8

The future of the Soviet
space programme

As the Soviet Union moves towards its fourth decade of space operations, clear strategic and technological trends are emerging. Within an overall geopolitical framework these trends embrace the military, commercial, and scientific-exploratory aspects of the Soviet space programme. A basic conclusion of these trends is that the Soviet presence in space is permanent and will steadily increase. This manned and unmanned presence in space will be dynamic and employ increasingly sophisticated technology.

The Politburo will continue its support of Soviet space efforts as an international means of demonstrating technological prowess, and as a positive domestic and foreign policy tool. Soviet space activities will be intended to 'fire the imagination' of the entire world. Such political support will remain steady and not demonstrate the uncertainty that has often characterized American and European efforts. The Soviet space programme has earned a formal position in the list of Soviet political priorities.

The space programme will be increasingly used to diffuse advanced technologies throughout other sectors of the Soviet economy. A steadily increasing emphasis will be placed on collaborative international space missions and commercial activities, which will result in the increased acquisition of advanced western technologies. Covert operations to obtain foreign technologies will also continue, and these will see direct input to the Soviet space programme. Barring catastrophic economic setbacks, the Soviet economy will continue the support, on a priorized basis, of the world's largest space programme. Serious reversals, perhaps a major manned accident, could make the programme temporarily falter, but not halt.

To date the Soviet space programme has been driven primarily by fundamental military requirements, and this underlying motivation will continue into the future. The military space imperative, with its corresponding marshalling of technological and economic resources and efficient organization, has been a primary factor in the overall success of Soviet space efforts. This is simply because in the Soviet Union few, if any, organizations are more efficiently managed than the military. Regardless of a future successful liberal restructuring of the Soviet economy, the Ministry of Defence, and in particular the Strategic Rocket Forces, the Air Force, and the Air Defence Forces (BMD), will continue to play important roles in the Soviet space programme. These roles will be analogous to the increasingly dominant influence of the USAF and SDI in American space efforts. The distinctions between 'defence' and 'space' budgets and organizations will become increasingly obscure. However, while in the past space technology development was dependent upon the military, in the future the military will become increasingly dependent upon space technology. As such, the Soviet space programme will be of primary importance in the maintenance and expansion of the Soviet Union's status as a first-class world power. This will be accomplished through the direct control, exploration, and commercial-scientific exploitation of outer space.

Soviet military space systems are currently integrated within an overall cohesive combined arms doctrine in support of conventional and strategic forces. These forces are structured to assist offensive land, sea and air operations, with an emphasis on supporting Soviet terrestrial objectives. However, as large-scale commercial and scientific space stations, habitats, and 'colonies' are developed by the Soviets and others in and beyond NEO, military activities related purely to 'war in space' and 'frontier control' will see increasing importance. Current Soviet ASAT and 'spacefighter' developments are a step in this direction. In the future it is likely that space-based BMD systems will eventually predominate over land-based ICBMs and other ballistic weapons. This will be even more probable if arms control negotiations result in a significant reduction of such offensive systems. In this scenario, the Strategic Rocket Forces would evolve into a true military space force. Current Soviet BMD activities are also supportive of such developments, as is the likely deployment of some future SDI-derived American BMD system.

It is now more likely, technically and politically, that the Soviets will embark upon large-scale commercial-scientific space activities such as SPSS, massive space stations/colonies and lunar resource bases, than the United States or western Europe. Such massive projects fit well within the Communist concept of Man's continuing economic progression, and are technically within the Soviets' grasp through the use of systems such as the Energia HLV. Co-operative commercial space activities will provide a complementary balance to, but not displace, the military space imperative. Soviet commercial activities will see increasing acceptance in the west and, eventually, even American technology transfer restrictions could be eased. In the long run the Soviets could face the stiffest commercial space competition from the Japanese who are now laying the ground-work for significant expansion in this direction.

Technologically Soviet space systems will see a continuous evolution and will eventually approach western standards of quality. The launch systems that are under development and entering service today — Energia, Cyclone MLV, space-plane, and space shuttle — will see continued upgrading and use well into the first two decades of the next century. Near the year 2000 older systems such as Proton and Soyuz will be gradually phased out after almost four decades of use. Technological improvements will allow Soviet weight-to-orbit to double and then quadruple from current levels by the turn-of-the-century. This could allow the deployment of extremely large manned space stations with hundreds of crew members and space-based BMD systems. It is almost a certainty that the Soviets will be the first to achieve a truly permanently manned presence in space. In addition, Soviet technological breakthroughs such as advanced nuclear or other propulsion systems, heavier HLVs, or single-stage-to-orbit space-planes should not be discounted for early in the next century.

It is likely that the Soviet Union will also maintain its leadership position in space science and exploration into the next century. These efforts will encourage, but not be dependent upon, international co-operation. It is now probable that the first humans to visit Mars and beyond will be Soviets. The Soviet colonies that will eventually be based on the Moon and Mars and in space will be fitting conclusions to the early prophecies of Konstantin Tsiolkovskii.

Appendix A

Chronology of Soviet space milestones

DATE[1]	EVENT(S)	DESCRIPTION
27 August 1957	SS-6 'Sapwood'	First[2] ICBM flight at intercontinental distances; liquid oxygen and hydro-carbon fuel engines
4 October 1957	Sputnik 1	First[2] artificial satellite
3 November 1957	Sputnik 2	World's second artificial satellite carrying first terrestrial creature in orbit: the dog Laika
2 January 1959 to 9 August 1976	Luna 1 to Luna 24	Unmanned lunar exploration programme that included three soil return missions and two Lunokhod exploratory rover missions
12 February 1961 to present	Venera 1 to Vega 1 and 2	Venusian exploration programme including landers, balloons, and remote sensing satellites
12 April 1961	Vostok 1	First human in orbit — Cosmonaut Yuri Gagarin; mission of one orbit lasting one hour and forty-eight minutes
6–7 August 1961	Vostok 2	First one-day orbital flight by Cosmonaut Gherman Titov
1 September 1961	Nuclear weapon test in space	A 58-megaton H-bomb was detonated by the Soviets at NEO — the largest nuclear explosion in history
26 April 1962	Cosmos 4	First military satellite; used to measure radia-tion levels resulting

		from nuclear tests; also, first satellite to be recovered
11–15 August 1962	Vostok 3 and 4	First multiple manned vehicle space mission
1 November 1962 to 9 August 1973	Mars 1 to 7	First Soviet unmanned Martian exploration series
14–19 June 1963	Vostok 5 and 6	Second multiple mission; Vostok 6 carried the world's first space woman, Cosmonaut Valentina Tereshkova
30 January 1964	Elecktron 1 and 2	First multiple pay-load launch; used to study the Van Allen Radiation Belt and the Earth's magnetic field
12–13 October 1964	Voskhod 1	First three-man space-craft flight, and first flight by a physician
18–19 March 1965	Voskhod 2	First manned space walk EVA performed by Cosmonaut Alexei Leonov
17 September 1966	Cosmos U-1	First offensive fractional orbit bombardment system (FOBS) test
23 April 1967	Soyuz 1	First flight of this manned series; ended tragically with the death of Cosmonaut Vladimir Komarov during re-entry
27 October 1967	Cosmos 185	First manoeuvrable anti-satellite (ASAT) test
27–30 October 1967	Cosmos 186 and 188	First automatic docking between two unmanned satellites
27 December 1967	Cosmos 198	First nuclear-powered

		radar ocean surveillance satellite (RORSAT)
15–22 September 1968	Zond 5	First spacecraft to circumnavigate the Moon and return safely to Earth
23 September 1968	Cosmos 243	First satellite to study heat emissions from the Earth and its atmosphere
26 December 1968	Cosmos 262	First satellite to study vacuum ultra-violet and soft X-ray radiation from the stars, Sun, and upper Earth atmosphere
14–18 January 1969	Soyuz 4 and 5	First manned docking followed by space-walk transfer of two cosmonauts from one vehicle to the other; in effect a rehearsal for a space rescue mission
July 1969	HLV explosion	Destruction of first-generation heavy lift vehicle on launch pad, with likely extensive loss of life and damage to facilities; ended Soviet competition with the United States in the 'Moon Race'
11–18 October 1969	Soyuz 6, 7, and 8	First simultaneous orbiting and manoeuvring of three manned spacecraft
1 June 1970	Soyuz 9	First manned launch at night; long-duration orbit record of 18 days which surpassed the earlier US Gemini 7 record
19 April 1971	Salyut 1	First manned space station

6 June 1971	Soyuz 11	Death of crew during re-entry: Cosmonauts Georgi Dobrovolsky, Vladislav Volkov, and Victor Patsayev
19 September 1972	Cosmos 520	First operational ICBM early warning satellite
26 March 1974	Cosmos 637	First Soviet GEO satellite
17 July 1975	Apollo-Soyuz Test Project (Soyuz 19 and Apollo 18)	Docking of Soviet and American manned space-craft; first such joint mission
22 October 1975	Venera 9	First photographs sent from the surface of another planet (Venus)
25 November to 15 December 1975	Cosmos 782	Experimental bio-satellite containing the first US experiments flown on a Soviet spacecraft
29 September 1977 to 29 July 1982	Salyut 6	Second-generation Soviet space station; significant step towards the perma-nent manned occupation of space, and perhaps equal in cost and lasting importance to the US Apollo Programme
10 December 1977 to 16 March 1978	Soyuz 26/ Salyut 6	97-day mission of a two-man crew which broke the previous 84-day long-duration manned spaceflight record of the third US Skylab crew
20 January 1978	Prognoz 1	First dedicated robotic supply/fuel-tanker space vehicle; derived from basic Soyuz design and used for Salyut and Mir support
2 March 1978	Soyuz 28	First international space

		launch mission; Soviet mission commander Cosmonaut Alexei Gubarev accompanied by Czech 'cosmonaut-researcher' Vladimir Remek
15 June to 2 November 1978	Soyuz 29	Record 139-day mission of Cosmonauts Vladimir Kovalenok and Alexander Ivanchenkov on board Salyut 6
25 February to 19 August 1979	Soyuz 32 to 34/ Salyut 6	Record 175-day mission on board Salyut 6 by Cosmonauts Vladimir Lyakhov and Valery Ryumin
9 April to 11 October 1980	Soyuz 35 to 37/ Salyut 6	Record 185-day mission on board Salyut 6 by Cosmonauts Valery Ryumin and Leonid Popov (Ryumin was a mere 3 days short of spending a total of one year in space)
27 November 1980	Soyuz T-3/ Salyut 6	First use of a space-borne laser (helium-neon gas laser used for holographic photography)
19 June 1981	Cosmos 1267– Salyut 6 link-up	First orbital demonstration of the modular assembly of large space station elements
1 March 1982	Venera 13	First soil analysis of another planet (Venus)
19 April 1982 to present	Salyut 7	Continued development towards a permanently manned space station; extensive cosmonaut EVAs for repairs and modifications

123

13 May 1982	Salyut 7/Soyuz T-5/Soyuz T-7	Long-duration 211-day stay on board Salyut 7 by Cosmonauts Anatoliy Berezovoy and Valentin Lebedev; first use of a pilot micro-electronics material production system
3 June 1982	Cosmos 1374	Initial orbital test of the Soviet sub-scale space-plane; perhaps a dozen such tests have occurred up till 1988
2 March 1983	Cosmos 1443/ Salyut 7	First operational space station multi-purpose 'tug'; previous experimental missions of the 'Star' vehicle were Cosmos 929 in November 1978 and Cosmos 1267 which linked to Salyut 6 on 19 June 1981
27 September 1983	Soyuz T-10A	First launch-pad fire and explosion of a manned spacecraft; ejection escape tower suc-cessfully used to save crew
28 September 1983	Cosmos 1500	First side-looking radar all-weather ocean surveillance satellite
October 1983 to January 1984	Venera 15 and 16	First remote surface mapping of Venus by orbiting satellite terrain-mapping radars
8 February to 2 October 1984	Salyut 7/Soyuz T-10	Long-duration stay of 237 days on board Salyut 7 by Cosmonauts Leonid Kizim, Vladimir Solovyev, and Oleg Atkov

28 September 1984	Cosmos 1603	Largest Soviet ELINT satellite
April 1985	SL-16 'Cyclone' Medium Launch Vehicle	First sub-orbital test of new generation MLV; first orbital attempt believed to have occurred on 21 June 1985; now operational
11–15 June 1985	Vega 1 and 2	Delivery of lander-probes and French balloons to Venus
20 February 1986 to present	Mir space station	Third-generation space station; likely to become permanently manned after full expansion via modules
6–9 March 1986	Vega 1 and 2	Close encounters with Halley's Comet; first imagery of a cometary core
5–6 May 1986	Mir/Soyuz T-15/ Salyut 7	First station-to-station transfer; by Cosmonauts Leonid Kizim and Vladimir Solovyev
12 April 1987	Kvant/Mir	Kvant (Quantum) astrophysics module is linked to Mir in the first phase of space station expansion
15 May 1987	Energia (SL-W/ SL-X-17) Heavy Lift Vehicle	Maiden flight of new HLV; successful operation of first stage kerosen/oxygen strap-on boosters, and cryogenic second stage propulsion system; payload pod failed to reach NEO due to a failure of its integral propulsion system; most powerful rocket in history

| 25 July 1987 | Cosmos 1870 | Largest Earth resources/ocean surveillance multisensor platform (15–20 tonnes) |

Appendix B

Soviet ICBM Data

Notes:

mt — megaton

kt — kiloton

Throw-Weight — Deliverable pay-load of ICBM, dependent on range, launch azimuth, re-entry angles, and other variables

IOC — Initial Operational Capability

MRV — Multiple Re-entry Vehicle (cannot be targeted individually)

CEP — Circular Error Probability (circular area around a target within which a warhead has 50 per cent chance of landing)

SRV — Single Re-entry Vehicle

MIRV — Multiple Independently Targetable Re-entry Vehicle

Missile (variant)	IOC	Type/ generation	Stages	Powerplant	Launch mode	Length (metres)	Diameter (metres)	Range (km)	Warhead type	Number and yield	CEP (metres)	Throw-weight (kg)	Remarks
SS-7 SADDLER	1962	Heavy/2nd	2	Liquid	Silo	35	3.0	11,000	SRV	1x3.5 mt	1,850	1,820	None deployed after 1979
SS-8 SASIN	1963	Heavy/2nd	2	Storage liquid	—	25	2.75	10,000	SRV	1x2 mt	1,850	1,590	None deployed after 1979
SS-9 SCARP (MOD-1)	1965	Heavy/3rd	3	Liquid	—	35	3.0	12,000	SRV	1x20 mt	740	5,000	None deployed after 1981 as ICBM Carrier vehicle for FOBS, ASAT, RORSAT.
SS-9 SCARP (MOD-4)	1971	Heavy/3rd	3	Liquid	—	35	3.0	12,000	MRV	3x3.5 mt	1,850	5,680	Same as above.
SS-11 SEGO (MOD-1)	1973	Light/3rd	2	Liquid	Silo	20	2.5	10,000	SRV	1x950 kt	1,400	1,000	
SS-11 SEGO (MOD-3)	1973	Light/3rd	2	Storable	Silo	20	2.5	10,000	MRV	3x200 kt	1,110	1,135	

Missile (variant)	IOC	Type/ generation	Stages	Powerplant	Launch mode	Length (metres)	Diameter (metres)	Range (km)	Warhead type	Number and yield	CEP (metres)	Throw-weight (kg)	Remarks
SS-12 SCALEBOARD	1969	IRBM	2	Solid	Mobile	11	—	800	SRV	1×500 kt	—	—	MAZ-53 truck mounted
SS-13 SAVAGE	1969	Light/3rd	3	Solid	Silo	20	1.7	10,000	SRV	1,600 kt	1,850	800	Limited deployment; only 60 in 1983; similar to US Minuteman
SS-14 SCAMP	—	IRBM	2	Solid	Mobile	10.6	1.4	4,000	SRV	—	—	—	Mobile in container on tracked transporter; tested but not deployed
SS-16 SINNER	1978	Light/4th	3	Solid	Silo/ mobile	20	2.5	9,200	SRV	1×650 kt	480	980	Related to SS-20. MIRV and advanced navigation capability
SS-17 SPANKER (MOD-1)	1975	Light/4th	2	Storable liquid	Silo/ cold	24	2.5	10,000	MIRV	4×750 kt	480	2,740	Mod 1 and Mod 3 operational in 130 silos
SS-17 SPANKER (MOD-2)	1977	Light/4th	2	Storable liquid	Silo/ cold	24	2.5	11,000	SRV	1×6 mt	425	2,730	Operational in 20 silos
SS-17 SPANKER (MOD-3)	1986	Light/4th	2	Storable liquid	Silo/ cold	24	2.5	10,000	MIRV	4×750 kt	350	2,740	Improved CEP over Mod 1
SS-18 SATAN (MOD-1)	1974	Heavy/4th	2	Storable liquid	Silo/ cold	35	3.0	12,000	SRV	1×27 mt	425	7,560	Total of 300 SS-18 (all mods) deployed; 393 silos
SS-18 SATAN (MOD-2)	1976	Heavy/	2	Storable liquid	Silo/ cold	35	3.0	11,000	MIRV	8×900 kt	425	7,590	
SS-18 SATAN (MOD-3)	1977	Heavy/4th	2	Storable liquid	Silo/	35	3.0	16,000	SRV	1×20 mt	350	7,500	

Missile (variant)	IOC	Type/ generation	Stages	Powerplant	Launch mode	Length (metres)	Diameter (metres)	Range (km)	Warhead type	Number and yield	CEP (metres)	Throw-weight (kg)	Remarks
SS-18 SATAN (MOD-4)	1979	Heavy/4th	2	Storable liquid	Silo cold	35	3.0	11,000	MIRV	10x500 kt	260	7,590	Advanced guidance systems: hard target capability; growth potential beyond 10rv's
SS-19 STILETTO (MOD-1)	1975	Light/4th	2	Storable liquid	Silo	25	2.75	9,600	MIRV	6x550 kt	390	3,420	Hot launch, uses converted SS-11 silos
SS-19 STILETTO (MOD-2)	1978	Light/4th	2	Storable liquid	Silo	25	2.75	10,000	SRV	1x10 mt	260	3,180	
SS-19 STILETTO (MOD-3)	1980	Light/4th	2	Storable liquid	Silo	25	2.75	10,000	MIRV	6x550 kt	280	3,410	
SS-20 SABER	1977	IRBM	2	Solid	Mobile	16	1.7	5,000 7,000	SRV or MIRV	1x650 kt 1x50 kt 3x150 kt	700	550	Uses first two stages of SS-16; 441 deployed
SS-X-24 SCALPEL	1986	Light/5th	—	Solid	Mobile/ Silo/ cold	21	—	9,000	MIRV	10x100 kt	200	—	Rail mobile
SS-25	1987?	Light/5th	—	Solid	Mobile	18	—	9,000	SRV with MIRV Potential	1x550 kt	200	—	Road mobile deployment

Glossary

ABM — anti-ballistic missile
ADI — Air Defence Initiative (US)
ASAT — anti-satellite
ASTP — Apollo-Soyuz Test Project
BMD — ballistic missile defence
C^3I — command, control, communications, and intelligence
CEP — circular error probable
CIA — Central Intelligence Agency (US)
CPSU — Communist Party of the Soviet Union
CETI — communication with extraterrestrial intelligence
ELINT — electronic intelligence
EMP — electromagnetic pulse
EORSAT — electronic ocean reconnaissance satellite
ESA — European Space Agency
EVA — extra-vehicular activity
EW — electronic warfare
FOBS — fractional orbit bombardment system
GAO — General Accounting Office (US)
GAU — Main Artillery Directorate
GEO — geo-synchronous earth orbit
GLONASS — Global Navigation Satellite System
GNP — gross national product
GOSPLAN — State Planning Committee
GPU — Main Production Units
GRAU — Main Missile and Artillery Directorate
GRU — Chief Intelligence Directorate of the General Staff
HLV — heavy launch vehicle
ICBM — intercontinental ballistic missile
Inmarsat — International Maritime Satellite Organization
IOC — initial operating capability
IRBM — intermediate range ballistic missile
KGB — Committee for State Security
kt — kiloton
LSO — lunar surface orbit
MARV — manoeuvring re-entry vehicle
MeV — mega (million) electron volt
MHD — magnetohydrodynamics
MIRV — multiple independently targetable re-entry vehicle

MLV — medium launch vehicle

MOBS — multiple orbit bombardment system

MOM — Ministry of Machine Building

MRBM — medium-range ballistic missile

MRV — multiple re-entry vehicle

mt — megaton

NASA — National Aeronautics and Space Administration (US)

NATO — North Atlantic Treaty Organization

NEO — near earth orbit

NKVD — national security force (prior to KGB)

NLO — near lunar orbit

NORAD — North American Aerospace Defence (Command)

OTH — over-the-horizon (radar)

PKO — Anti-Cosmic (Anti-Satellite) Defence Forces

PRO — Anti-Missile Defence Forces

PVO — Strategic Air Defence Forces

RF — radio frequency

RFQ — radio frequency quadrapole

RORSAT — radar ocean reconnaissance satellite

RV — re-entry vehicle

SA — surface-to-air

SAC — Strategic Air Command (US7

SAR — synthetic aperture radar

SAINT — Satellite Intercept (Programme — US)

SALT — Strategic Arms Limitation Treaty/Talks

SDI — Strategic Defence Initiative (US)

SDIO — Strategic Defence Initiative Organization

SL — Soviet launcher

SLBM — submarine-launched ballistic missile

SPSS — solar power satellite system

SRF — Strategic Rocket Forces

SRV — single re-entry vehicle

TTZ — tactical technical task document

UN — United Nations

US — United States (of America)

USAF — United States Air Force

USSR — Union of Soviet Socialist Republics

VGK — Supreme High Command

VPK — Military Industrial Commission

Notes

1 HISTORICAL OVERVIEW

1 K.E. Tsiolkovskii (1967) 'Autobiography', in A.C. Clarke (ed.), *The Coming of the Space Age*, New York: Meredith Press, pp. 100–4.

2 W. Ley (1958) *Satellites, Rockets, and Outer Space*, New York: Signet Science Library, pp. 25–6.

3 R. Hutton (1981) *The Cosmic Chase*, New York: Mentor, pp. 15–16.

4 Quoted in I.S. Shklovskii and C. Sagan (1966) *Intelligent Life in the Universe*, New York: Dell, p. 8.

5 W. Shelton (1968) *Soviet Space Exploration: The First Decade*, New York: Washington Square Press, pp. 24–5.

6 J.E. Oberg (1981) *Red Star in Orbit*, New York: Random House, pp. 18–19.

7 M.N. Golovine (1962) *Conflict in Space*, New York: St Martin's Press, p. 54.

8 G.H. Stine (1981) *Confrontation in Space*, Englewood Cliffs, NJ: Prentice-Hall, pp. 29–33.

9 Shelton (1968) *Soviet Space Exploration: The First Decade*, pp. 41–4.

10 Marshal of the Soviet Union V.D. Sokolovskii (ed.) (1962) *Military Strategy* Moscow: Military Publishing House of the Ministry of Defence of the Soviet Union, 464 pp. Published in English as V.D. Sokolovskii (ed.) 1963 *Soviet Military Strategy*, Santa Monica, Calif: Rand Corporation.

11 From a speech delivered 22 January 1958 called 'Some aspects of international situation' in N. Khrushchev (1954) *For Victory in the Peaceful Competition with Capitalism*, Moscow: Foreign Languages Publishing House, pp. 30–8.

12 Shelton (1968) *Soviet Space Exploration: The First Decade*, p. 43.

13 Excellent detailed historical chronological reviews of Soviet unmanned space activities are contained in the US Library of Congress report, *Soviet Space Programs: 1976–80 (With Supplementary Data Through 1983), Unmanned Space Activities, Part 3*, and R. Turnill (1986) *Jane's Spaceflight Directory*, London: Jane's Publishing. For a Soviet account see Yu.I. Zaitsev (1974) *From Sputnik to Space Station*, translated by Group Captain A.E.C. York, British Library Lending Division.

14 Zaitsev (1974) *From Sputnik to Space Station*. See US Library of Congress report, *Soviet Space Programs: 1976–80 (With Supplementary Data Through 1983), Manned Space Programs and Space Life Sciences, Part 2*: Turnill (1986) *Jane's Spaceflight Directory*; Oberg (1981) *Red Star in Orbit*; W. Brzozowski (1982) 'Development of the Soviet space program', *AIAA Student Journal*, Spring: 3–13; and P. Pasavento (1986) 'Soviet Spaceflight comes of age', *New Scientist* 10 April: 44–7.

15 Although the benefits of this mission to the United States have been hotly debated, it was a follow-through to an agreement on the peaceful exploration of space signed by President Nixon and President Kosygin on 24 May 1972. Many in the west had doubted the mission would actually

occur, but the Soviets were attracted by possible technology transfer from the Americans, and improved management techniques in such areas as quality assurance. For the USA, ASTP provided political benefits, information on the Soviet space programme, and some valuable manned spaceflight activity, using old Apollo hardware, between the completion of Skylab and the start of space shuttle flights.

2 SPACE PROGRAMME INFRASTRUCTURE

1 See M.L. Harvey, L. Goure and V. Prokofieff (1977) *Science and Technology as an Instrument of Soviet Policy*, University of Miami: Centre for Advanced International Studies. In particular their first section on Soviet perceptions on the use of science and technology in the class struggle between the communist and capitalist systems.

2 G. Taubes and G. Garelik (1986) 'Soviet science', *Discover*, August: 36–59.

3 H.D. Balzer (1985) 'Is less more? Soviet science in the Gorbachev era', *Issues in Science and Technology*, Summer: 29–46. Interesting anecdotes relating to the inherent problems encountered within the Soviet military research and development bureaucracy are found in A. Cockburn (1982) *The Threat: Inside the Soviet Military Machine*, New York: Random House.

4 P. Kelly (1986) 'How the USSR broke into the nuclear club', *New Scientist*, 8 May: 32–5.

5 E. Kozicharow (1984) 'Soviets realign research efforts', *Aviation Week and Space Technology*, 7 May: 14–16.

6 P. Jefferson and J. Benson (1980) 'Washington scene', *Astronautics and Aeronautics*, November: 17–18.

7 P. Mann (1984) 'U.S. Assesses technology leadership', *Aviation Week and Space Technology*, 23 April: 28; H. Simmons (1984) 'Defence technology: there goes the gap', *Aerospace America*, May: 12–15; R.J. Smith (1986) 'U.S. tops Soviets in key weapons technology', *Science*, 7 March: 1,063–4.

8 P.J. Klass (1980) 'Soviet microcircuits found trailing U.S.', *Aviation Week and Space Technology*, 8 December: 64–7; US Defense Department (1981) *Soviet Military Power*, Washington, DC: US Government Printing Office, pp. 74–5.

9 Anon. (1986) 'Why Moscow covets U.S. supercomputers', *Science Digest*, July: 41.

10 Anon. (1986) 'Soviets develop compact digital image processing system', *Aviation Week and Space Technology*, 17 November: 49.

11 US Defense Department (1981) *Soviet Military Power*, pp. 80–1.

12 B.M. Greenley, jr (1985) 'Soviets target U.S. companies, universities for new technologies', *Aviation Week and Space Technology*, 30 September: 86–90; S.M. Meyer, (1986) 'The Soviet "Spy Gaps" ', *IEEE Spectrum* July: 69.

13 D.M. North (1986) 'Soviet advances spurring western aircraft upgrades', *Aviation Week and Space Technology*, 21 July: 45; Anon. (1986) 'Soviet acquisition of western avionics technology concerns defence dept', *Aviation Weeek and Space Technology* 21 July: 79.

14 US Defense Department (1981) *Soviet Military Power*, p. 9; Anon. (1984) 'NATO cites Soviet military funding slowdown', *Aviation Week and Space Technology*, 13 February: 140; B.M. Greenley, jr (1985) 'CIA, defence intelligence diverge on Soviet arms spending growth', *Aviation Week and Space Technology*, 18 March: 101–4; Anon. (1986) 'Soviet defence spending reaches 3% annual growth', *Aviation Week and Space Technology*, 24 February: 91.

15 M. Heylin (1984) 'Report outlines scope of massive growing Soviet military R & D, *C & EN*, 30 April: 14–15.

16 Simmons (1984) 'Defence technology', p. 15.

17 C.S. Sheldon II (1968) *Review of the Soviet Space Program*, New York: McGraw-Hill, 83–4. US Library of Congress *Soviet Space Programs: 1976–80, Part One*, pp. 334–5.

18 ibid; R. Turnill (1984) *Jane's Spaceflight Directory* London: Jane's Publishing, p. 5; Brigadier General R.R. Rankine, jr, USAF (1987) 'The military and space . . . yesterday, today and tomorrow', *JRUSI*, June: 8–9; W. Shelton (1965) *Soviet Space Exploration: The First Decade*, New York: Washington Square Press, pp. 40–1; Bergaust (1969) *The Russians in Space*, New York: G.P. Putnam & Sons, pp. 28–35.

19 P.N. James (1974) *Soviet Conquest From Space* New York: Arlington House Publishers, pp. 55–68; US Library of Congress, *Soviet Space Programs: 1976–80, Part One*, pp. 8–9 and 307–28.

20 Anon. (1985) 'News digest', *Aviation Week and Space Technology*, 4 November: p. 28; V.Rich (1985) 'New Soviet space agency is formed', *Nature*, 7 November: 7; J.M. Lenorovitz (1986) 'Soviet aims include expanding international space participation and streamlining management', *Commercial Space* Spring: 37–8; Anon. (1986) 'Soviets assign Glavkosmos primary space program role', *Aviation Week and Space Technology*, 13 October: 19.

21 J. Maddox (1986) 'A child's guide to Soviet science', *Nature*, 13 March: 105.

22 James (1974) *Soviet Conquest from Space*, pp. 69–80; R.D. Ward (1981) 'Soviet practise in designing and procuring military aircraft', *Astronautics and Aeronautics*, September: 24–38; Executive Office of the President, Office of Science and Technology Policy (1982) *Aeronautical Research and Technology Policy Volume II: Final Report*, November, pp. II-2–II-14.

23 S.B. Kramer (1982) 'Letters to the editor', *Aviation Week and Space Technology*, 11 October: 148.

24 Anon. (1983) 'Soviets construct new space facilities', *Aviation Week and Space Technology*, 21 March: 21; Anon. (1984) 'Shuttle crew photographs Soviet sites', *Aviation Week and Space Technology*, 9 January: 19; and Anon. (1986) 'Soviet space shuttle facilities at Tyuratam imaged by French spot', *Aviation Week and Space Technology*, 1 September: 42–3.

25 B.M. Jasani (1978) *Outer Space — Battlefield of the Future?*, London: Taylor & Francis, p. 36.

26 J.E. Oberg (1981) *Red Star in Orbit*, New York: Random House, pp. 150–61; J.M. Lenorovitz, (1986) 'Soviet cosmonauts training at Star City', *Aviation Week and Space Technology*, 9 August: 44–6; M. Gerard (1983)

'A peek at Start City', *Astronautics and Aeronautics*, February: 59; *Reuter* (1986) 'Foreign reporters receive rare glimpse of cosmonauts', 8 April.

3 MILITARY SPACE

1 For an elaboration of these factors see: R.E. Walters (1974) *The Nuclear Trap: An Escape Route*, Harmondsworth: Penguin; Ambassador H.- G. Wieck (1984) 'The Soviet Threat', *Proceedings*, Sea Link Special Issue: 26–35; B.D. Bruins (1984) 'Understanding the Soviet Union', *Proceedings*, September: 66–71; C.N. Donnelly (1985) 'The human factor in Soviet military policy', *Military Review*, March: 12–22; Major E.F. Meis III, US Army (1986) 'Militarism in Russia: From imperial roots to the Soviet Union', *Military Review*, July: 28–37; Z.Brzezinski (1986) *Game Plan: A Geostrategic Framework for the Conduct of the US–Soviet Contest*, Boston, Mass: Atlantic Monthly Press; J. Sherr (1986) 'Soviet policy: recurring predicaments, enduring challenges', *Journal of the Royal United Institute for Defence Studies*, June: 49–54.

2 C.S. Gray (1984) 'International order and American power', *Air University Review*, September-October: 26–34; C.S. Gray (1984) 'Planning for U.S. Security interests', *Proceedings*, December: 37–43; C.S. Gray (1985) 'Comparative strategic culture', *Parameters*, 14, 4; 26–33.

3 V.D. Sokolovskii (ed.) (1963) *Soviet Military Strategy*, Santa Monica, Calif: Rand Corporation, p. 297. (Original Soviet edition published 1962.)

4 ibid., p. 313, original emphasis.

5 ibid., p. 99.

6 ibid., p. 305.

7 Brigadier J. Hemsley (1986) 'The influence of technology upon Soviet operational doctrine', *Journal of the Royal United Services Institute for Defence Studies*, June: 21–8.

8 Wieck (1984) 'The Soviet threat', p. 28.

9 V. Suvorov (1984) *Inside the Soviet Army*, London: Granada, pp. 243–57. Suvorov outlines the standard Soviet offensive scenario of five stages, the first of which is a nuclear pre-emptive strike on all military targets.

10 Sokolovskii (1963) *Soviet Military Strategy*, pp. 293–4. The application of advanced technologies to military capabilities is also repeatedly stressed in more current Soviet military literature. For example, see Colonel V. Bondarenko, (1986) 'Scientific–technical progress and military affairs', *Communist of the Armed Force*, November, 21.

11 S.T. Possony and J.E. Pournelle (1970) *The Strategy of Technology*, Cambridge: Dunellen, pp. 4 –18.

12 ibid., p. 4.

13 ibid., pp. 22–3 and 43.

14 J.G. Hines and G.F. Kraus (1986) 'Soviet strategies for military competition', *Parameters*, 16, 3: 26–31.

15 F. Dyson (1979) *Disturbing the Universe*, New York: Harper & Row, p. 136.

16. Sokolovskii (1963) *Soviet Military Strategy*, p. 427.

17 See, for example, R.D. Humble (1982) 'Space warfare in perspective', *Air University Review*, July-August: 81–6; and R.D. Humble (1982) 'On the military use of space', *Journal of the Royal United Services Institute for Defence Studies*, September: 38–45.

18 R. Turnill (1985) *Jane's Spaceflight Directory*, London: Jane's Publishing, p. 1; C.S. Gray and B.R. Schneider (1984) 'The Soviet military space program', *Signal*, December: 69.

19 Turnill (1985) *Jane's Spaceflight Directory*, p. 146; Yu.I. Zaitsev (1974) *From Sputnik to Space Station*, British Library Lending Division, pp. 11–12.

20 C. Covault (1986) 'Soviet military space flight fails, warning satellite placed in wrong orbit', *Aviation Week and Space Technology*, 27 October: 24–5.

21 K.J. Stein (1984) 'Current technologies could aid in implementing Reagan's SDI policy', *Aviation Week and Space Technology*, 10 December: 76.

22 R.P. Linville (1986) 'Space and Soviet military planning', *Space Policy*, August: 235–9.

23 US Defense Intelligence Agency Report, *Soviet Military Space Doctrine*, quoted in Commander B.L. Valley, US Navy, (1985) 'The ultimate defence', *Proceedings*, February: 33.

24 Major L.A. Roe and Major D.H. Wise (1986) 'Space power is land power: the Army's role in space', *Military Review*, January: 5–7.

25 Anon. (1982) 'Soviets stage integrated test of weapons', *Aviation Week and Space Technology*, 28 June: 20–1; Anon. (1983) 'Soviets integrating space in strategic war planning', *Aviation Week and Space Technology*, 14 March: 110–11; J. Oberg (1986) 'Beware the Soviet space arsenal', *New Scientist*, 1 May: 37.

26 *TRW Space Log 1984–1985*, 21; 32.

27 Hines and Kraus (1986) 'Soviet strategies for military competition', p. 28.

28 T. Wolfe (1979) *The Right Stuff*, New York: Farrar-Straus-Giroux, p. 72.

29 C. Brownlow (1967) 'Soviets prepare space weapon for 1968', *Aviation Week and Space Technology*, 13 November: 30–1.

30 D.C. Winston (1968) 'FOBS may widen SAC dispersal', *Aviation Week and Space Technology*, 10 June: 16–17.

31 See: Turnill (1985) *Jane's Spaceflight Directory*, pp. 240, 252; US Library of Congress, *Soviet Space Programs: 1976–1980, Part One*, pp. 105–9, and *Part Three*, pp. 1,094–101; and B.M. Jasani (1978) *Outer Space — Battlefield of the Future?*, London: Taylor & Francis, pp. 179–83.

32 R. Salkeld (1970) *War and Space*, Englewood Cliffs, NJ: Prentice-Hall.

33 C.A. Robinson, jr. (1981) 'Decisions reached on nuclear weapons', *Aviation Week and Space Technology*, 12 October: 18–23; C.A. Robinson, jr. (1982) 'USAF restudies orbital basing of MX', *Aviation Week and Space Technology*, 12 April: 83–9. Other American studies have proposed orbital basing schemes for Minuteman 3 and Trident 2.

34 Anon. (1983) 'Soviets integrating space in strategic war planning', p. 110; J.E. Oberg (1983) 'The elusive Soviet space plane', *OMNI*, September: pp. 124–9 and 143.

35 B.M. Jasani (1982) 'Space: battlefield of the future', *Futures*, October: 438.

36 D.L. Hafner (1980/81) 'Averting a Brobdingnagian skeet shoot', *International Security*, Winter: 46.

37 R.L. Garthoff (1984) 'ASAT arms control: still possible', *Bulletin of the Atomic Scientists*, August/September: 29–31.

38 J.E. Oberg (1986) *National Review*, 14 February: 25. Also see Oberg (1984) 'Weapons in orbit', *Science Digest*, April: 41–5 and 96–7, and Oberg (1986) 'Beware the Soviet space arsenal', *New Scientist*, 1 May: 36–9.

39 Turnill (1985) *Jane's Spaceflight Directory*, pp. 237–8 and 252; W.J. Durch (1985) 'Soviet ASAT outlook', *Aerospace America*, January: 130–1; J. Ethell (1985) 'To kill or not to kill satellites', *Aerospace America*, November: 10–13.

40 C. Covault (1980) 'Universe Red', *OMNI*, August: 53.

41 Anon. (1981) 'Soviets continue aggressive space drive', *Aviation Week and Space Technology*, 9 March: 88–9; Anon. (1986) 'Soviets outspending U.S. on space by $3–4 billion', *Aviation Week and Space Technology*, 19 July: 28–9; Anon. (1984) 'USAF pushes survivability of satellites', *Aviation Week and Space Technology*, 24 September: 71–2; R.R. Ropelewski (1985) 'Congressional office warns arms pacts will not halt ASAT threat', *Aviation Week and Space Technology*, 30 September: 20–2.

42 Anon. (1982) 'Soviets stage integrated test of weapons', pp. 20–1; Anon. (1983) 'Soviet threat in space said to be on rise', *Aviation Week and Space Technology*, 16 May: 46–7; Anon. (1984) 'U.S. urged to negotiate treaty based upon freedom of space', *Aviation Week and Space Technology*, 28 May: 118; C.A. Robinson, jr (1984) 'Strategic defence group speeds efforts', *Aviation Week and Space Technology*, 11 June: 17; US Office of Technology Assessment (1984) *Arms Control in Space: Workshop Proceedings*, Washington, DC: US Congress, May, pp. 10 and 42–3.

43 G.H. Stine (1981) *Confrontation in Space*, Englewood Cliffs, NJ; Prentice-Hall, p. 68; P.J. Klass (1986) 'Soviets expected to seek ban on spaceborne antisatellite arms', *Aviation Week and Space Technology*, 17 December: 22.

44 J.E. Oberg (1984) 'Pearl Harbor in space', *OMNI*, July: 43–4 and 64–73.

45 Anon. (1984) 'Cosmos 1,603 conducts space manoeuvres', *Aviation Week and Space Technology*, 22 October: 24.

46 Anon. (1981) 'Washington roundup', *Aviation Week and Space Technology*, 26 October: 15; Anon. (1981) 'Washington roundup', *Aviation Week and Space Technology*, 2 November: 15; Anon. (1981) 'Washington roundup', *Aviation Week and Space Technology*, 30 November: 17; Anon. (1982) 'Soviet military programs in space move forward', *Aviation Week and Space Technology*, 8 March: 106.

47 Anon. (1982) 'Intelligence estimate revealed unintentionally', *Aviation Week and Space Technology*, 8 March: 272; Anon. (1982) 'Burke assesses Soviet laser capability', *Aviation Week and Space Technology*, 3 May: 13; L. David (1983) 'Soviet military power: a Pentagon view', *Space World*, August-September: 4–6; Robinson (1984) 'Strategic defence group speeds efforts', p. 17; J. Gotting (1985) 'Space weapons and intelligence satellites', *Armed Forces*, June: 222–5.

48 Anon. (1984) 'Washington roundup', *Aviation Week and Space Technology*, 9 July: 13; Reuter (1986) 'German paper says Soviet rays have blinded U.S. spy satellites', 25 October.

49 Turnill (1985) *Jane's Spaceflight Directory*, p. 252.

50 Oberg (1986) 'Beware the Soviet space arsenal', p. 39.

51 US Office of Technology Assessment (1984) *Arms Control in Space: Workshop Proceedings*, p. 27.

52 F.X. Kane (1982) 'Anti-satellite systems and U.S. options', *Strategic Review*, Winter: 56–64.

53 C. Covault (1983) 'Soviet nuclear spacecraft poses reentry danger', *Aviation Week and Space Technology*, 10 January: 18–19; Anon. (1985) 'Soviet Nuclear-powered satellite boosts naval surveillance capability', *Aviation Week and Space Technology*, 19 August: p. 18; G.O'Lone (1986) 'USAF official calls Soviet satellites threat to U.S. carrier battle groups', *Aviation Week and Space Technology*, 29 September: 20; Turnill (1985) *Jane's Spaceflight Directory*, p. 254.

54 R.S. Cooper (1986) 'No sanctuary: a defence perspective on space', *Issues in Science and Technology*, Spring: 43 and 45.

55 Oberg (1984) 'Weapons in orbit', p. 43.

56 N.L. Johnson (1986) 'Nuclear power supplies in orbit', *Space Policy*, August: 223–33; Anon. (1986) 'Radioactive space debris study cites hazards to satellites, Earth', *Aviation Week and Space Technology*, 22 September: 19–20.

57 Anon. (1984) 'Soviet cosmos spacecraft providing land, sea imagery', *Aviation Week and Space Technology*, 19 November 212–13.

58 United Nations Department for Disarmament Affairs (1983) *The Implications of Establishing an International Satellite Monitoring Agency*, New York: United Nations, pp. 12–13.

59 Anon. (1982) 'Soviet satellite orbiting over South Atlantic', *Aviation Week and Space Technology*, 26 April: 24; Anon. (1982) 'Soviet military reconnaissance satellite missions accelerate', *Aviation Week and Space Technology*, 3 May: 22; Anon. (1982) 'Soviets launch another surveillance satellite', *Aviation Week and Space Technology*, 10 May: 24; Anon. (1982) 'Falklands reconnaissance improved by Soviet Union', *Aviation Week and Space Technology*, 24 May: 20; Anon. (1982) 'Soviets again boost Falklands reconnaissance', *Aviation Week and Space Technology*, 31 May: 20; Anon. (1982) 'Soviets launch ocean surveillance satellite', *Aviation Week and Space Technology*, 7 June: 16.

60 Anon. (1987) 'Soviet Union takes lead in manned space operations', *Aviation Week and Space Technology*, 9 March: 132.

61 Anon. (1985) 'USSR boosts reconnaissance capabilities', *Aviation Week and Space Technology*, 21 January: 15; Turnill (1985) *Jane's Spaceflight Directory*, p. 253; S.M. Meyer (1986) 'The Soviet "Spy Gaps" ', *IEEE Spectrum*, July: 67–8.

62 Meyer (1986) 'The Soviet "Spy Gaps" ', p. 68.

63 Anon. (1985) 'Soviets orbit large new military electronic intelligence satellite', *Aviation Week and Space Technology*, 14 January: 19–20.

64 K. Freeman (1984) 'Satellites and anti-satellites (part 2)', *Armed Forces*, September: 330.

65 David (1983) 'Soviet military power: a Pentagon view', p. 6.

4 THE STRATEGIC ROCKET FORCES

1 Anon. (1984) 'Washington roundup', *Aviation Week and Space Technology*, 30 January: 15; J. Ethell (1985) 'Biochemical warfare — new no-man's land?', *Aerospace America*, September: 12. This capability to attack vast population centres and strategic targets such as missile and space bases would add a new, if horrific, dimension to Soviet chemical warfare.

2 For an interesting survey and analysis of the Russian experience with artillery and missiles from the imperial era to contemporary Soviet times, see C. Bellam (1986) *Red God of War: Soviet Artillery and Rocket Forces*, London: Brassey's Defence Publishers; J. Zalonga (1976) 'Soviet strategic missile development and production', *Jane's Defence Weekly*, 30 May: 1,063–4. Others have commented that many contemporary Soviet commanders consider tactical nuclear weapons simply as a form of 'heavier artillery', and the western disinclination for the use of such weapons is indicative of a 'sissy warfare' mentality.

3 Commander-in-Chief of the Strategic Rocket Forces, Chief Marshal of Artillery V.F. Tolubko (1984) 'Today is rocket forces and artillery day: the Motherland's reliable shield', *Pravda*, 19 November.

4 First Deputy Commander-in-Chief of the Strategic Rocket Forces, Colonel General Yu.A. Yashin (1984) 'The Motherland's reliable shield: 19 November — rocket forces and artillery day', *Izvestiya*, 19 November.

5 US Defense Department (1981) *Soviet Military Power*, Washington, DC: US Government Printing Office, pp. 54–5; V. Suvorov (1982) *Inside the Soviet Army*, London: Granada, pp. 91–9; E.S. Williams (1987) ' "Restructuring" and the SRF', *Armed Forces*, April: 175 and 180.

6 C.D. Blacker (1985) 'Defending missiles, not people: hard-site defense', *Issues in Science and Technology*, Fall: 40–1. In contrast, most US ICBM's are located at some distance from major population centres.

7 Anon. (1983) 'The land based strategic missile balance', *War Machine*, 1, 2:23.

8 W.C. Green (1987) 'Arms race: stepping up the Soviet NBC ladder', *Nuclear, Biological and Chemical Defence and Technology International*, 2, 1; 18. The US ICBM force currently consists of 1,000 Minuteman missiles and, eventually, 50 to 100 or more MX Peacekeeper missiles. The 'Midgetman' mobile ICBM is currently under development.

9 See C.A. Robinson, Jr (1980) 'Soviets testing new generation of ICBMs', *Aviation Week and Space Technology*, 3 November: 28–9; C.A. Robinson, jr (1981) 'U.S. upgrading its strategic arsenal', *Aviation Week and Space Technology*, 9 March: 27; B. Stewart (1981) 'MX and the counterforce problem: a case for silo deployment', *Strategic Review*, Summer: 17; C.A. Robinson, jr (1981) 'Soviet Union defensive buildup detailed by Weinberger', *Aviation Week and Space Technology*, 5 October: pp. 21–2; C.A. Robinson, jr (1982) 'Soviet force investment shifting strategic balance', *Aviation Week and Space Technology*, 22 February: 23–4; C.A. Robinson, jr (1982) 'Emphasis grows on nuclear defence', *Aviation Week and Space Technology*, 8 March: 27.

10 W.T. Lee and R.F. Staar (1986) *Soviet Military Policy Since World War II*, Stanford, Calif: Hoover Institution Press. The authors argue that the

Soviets did not develop MIRVs as a reaction to US developments, but rather as the most practical way to 'service' an expanding list of targets. The authors also argue that in general the Soviets develop and deploy nuclear weapons to obtain a superior warfighting capability.

11 C.A. Robinson, jr (1982) 'Administration pushes ICBM defence', *Aviation Week and Space Technology*, 11 October: 115.

12 Anon. (1983) 'Only 10%–35% U.S. ICBM's would survive Soviet attack now', *High Frontier Newsletter*, August: 6.

13 C.A. Appleby (1986) 'Mobile missiles: invincible and unverifiable?' Nuclear, Biological, Chemical Defence and Technology International, May: 28–9.

14 For a thorough discussion of this issue see A.G.B. Metcalf (1981) 'Missile accuracy — the need to know', *Strategic review*, Summer: 5–8; General R.T. Marsh, USAF (1982) 'Strategic missiles debated: missile accuracy — we do know!', *Strategic Review*, Spring: 35–7 and 42–3; J.E. Anderson (1982) 'Strategic missiles debated: missile vulnerability — what you can't know!' *Strategic Review*, Spring: 38–42; Dr S. Smith (1985) 'Problems of assessing missile accuracy', *Journal of the Royal United Services Institute for Defence Studies*, December: 35–40. Missile warhead lethality is a combination of yield in megatons and CEP in distance to target (circular error probable simply describes the radius of a circle, the centre of which is the intended target, within which warheads are likely to hit). CEP is dependent upon accurate missile guidance and control to its intended target even in very hostile environments. Soviet and US ICBMs have not been tested in a North Polar ballistic trajectory that would be used in actual war, hence uncertainty still remains as to ultimate accuracy. However, advanced manoeuvring re-entry vehicle (MARV) and terminal guidance technologies such as those employed on the US Pershing II could soon achieve CEPs of 0 (i.e. direct hits).

15 L.R. Sykes and D.M. Davis (1987) 'The yields of Soviet strategic weapons', *Scientific American*, January: 29–37.

16 M. McGwire (1987) 'Why the Soviets want arms control', *Technology Review*, February/March: 36–45.

17 W.D. Henderson (1982) 'Space-based lasers: ultimate ABM system?', *Astronautics and Aeronautics*, May: 51; M. Nincic (1986) 'Can the U.S. trust the U.S.S.R?', *Scientific American*, April: 41.

18 Suvorov (1982) *Inside the Soviet Army*, p. 169. Suvorov refers to the SS-20 as the UR-100 'universal rocket'. He also describes a SAM, the S-200, which supposedly has an ABM capability.

19 S.T. Possony and J.E. Pournelle (1970) *The Strategy of Technology*, Cambridge: Dunellen, pp. 135–7. The US 'Project Janus' was a case in point.

20 B.D. Berkowtiz (1986) 'Commentary: coming constraints in arms control agreements — approaching the limits of feasible regulation', *Science, Technology and Human Values*, Winter: 21.

21 J.D. Morrocco (1987) 'Soviet strategic force upgrade paces U.S. modernization effort', *Aviation Week and Space Technology*, 9 March: 31.

22 D.S. Meyers (1986) 'Soviet proposals on the militarization of space', *Space Policy*, August: 240–52.

23 Anon. (1986) 'Star peace', *New Scientist*, 19 June: 25; Anon. (1986) 'Soviets propose world space body to promote projects', *Reuter*, 13 June;

Anon. (1987) 'Satellite inspection proposed', *Reuter*, 18 March.

24 Anon. (1986) 'Analysis: arms control', *RUSI News Brief*, October: 6-8.

25 Anon. (1987) ' "Turning point" sought in talks', *Associated Press*, 14 January.

26 P. Mann (1985) 'Reagan rules out ending SDI effort in exchange for Soviet missile cuts', *Aviation Week and Space Technology*, 30 September: 93-7.

27 Anon. (1987) 'Ballistic missile proposal killed by Soviets, U.S. says', *Associated Press*, 10 April.

28 Anon. (1985) 'Aerospace spotlight', *Aerospace America*, May: 1.

29 See the Committee of Nuclear Scientists for Peace and Against the Nuclear Threat (1984) *Strategic and International-Political Consequences of Creating a Space-based Anti-Missile System Using Directed-Energy Weapons*, Moscow: Institute for Space Research of the USSR Academy of Sciences, April; Y.P. Velikhov (1984) 'Effect on strategic stability', *Bulletin of the Atomic Scientists*, May: 12S-5S; Y.P. Velikhov (1985) *The Night After: Climatic and Biological Consequences of a Nuclear War*, Moscow: Mir Publishing House; Soviet Scientists' Committee for the Defence of Peace Against Threat (1986) *Weaponry in Space: The Dilemma of Security*, Moscow: December; R. Sagdeyev and S. Rodinov (1986) 'To the question of the strategic and economic consequences of SDI', *World Economics and International Relations*, May.

30 D.E. Fink (1986) 'SDI prevails at Reykjavik', *Aviation Week and Space Technology*, 20 October: 23.

31 C.A. Robinson, jr (1982) 'GAO pushing accelerated laser program', *Aviation Week and Space Technology*, 12 April: 16-17; J.Y. Young, jr (1986) 'Key objectives for the strategic defence initiative, *AIAA Student Jr*, Fall: 7.

32 Anon. (1987) 'SDI watch', *National Review*, 13 March: 17; W. Flora (1984) 'Administration defends ABM program', *Aviation Week and Space Technology*, 14 May: 23. The reduction of 70-90 per cent of total re-entry vehicle payload and a greatly reduced decoy payload, for example, would be equivalent to a 70-90 per cent effective boost-phase defence against current ICBMs.

33 Anon. (1986) 'Marshall Institute claims OTA overrates Soviet deterrent to layered defence', *Aviation Week and Space Technology*, 24 March: 28-9.

5 BALLISTIC MISSILE DEFENCE

1 J.C. McCrery, Defense Intelligence Officer for Strategic Programs, United States Defense Intelligence Agency, addressing the American Institute of Aeronautics and Astronautics Annual Conference, 'Aerospace '87', Washington, DC, 29 April 1987.

2 U. Ra'anan and R.H. Shultz, jr (1987) 'Oral history: a neglected dimension of Sovietology', *Strategic Review* Spring: 64-7.

3 W.C. Green (1987) 'Arms race: stepping up the Soviet NBC ladder', *Nuclear, Biological and Chemical Defence and Technology International* (1987 Yearbook), pp. 16-17.

4 Anon. (1987) 'Arms control agency challenges Nunn's contention on legality of testing kinetic systems', *Aviation Week and Space Technology*, 23 March: 29; D. Quayle (1987) 'Putting the spotlight on the Soviets', *Defence News*, 27 April: 20.

5 M.F. Altfeld (1986) 'Strategic defence and the "Cost-Exchange ratio" ', *Strategic Review*, Fall: 21–6.

6 For a good review of Soviet BMD developments see J. Pike, 'Assessing the Soviet ABM programme', in E.P. Thompson (ed.) (1985) *Star Wars*, Harmondsworth: Penguin, pp. 50–67. Pike tends to be rather sceptical of Soviet BMD capabilities.

7 This system has recently been upgraded with Henhouse early warning radars, Dog/Cat House phased-array battle management radars, and 1960s-era Try-Add battle engagement radars. The latter system is being replaced by two types of hybrid phased-array/mechanically steered radars — the Flat Twin to track incoming RVs, and the Pawn Shop for missile interceptor target intercept. The Flat Twin is a modular radar that can be erected on a prepared site within six to eight weeks. The Pawn Shop can be deployed within several weeks. The large Pushkino battle-management phased-array radar under construction near Moscow will supplement the Cat House and Dog House radars for long-range (SH-4) interceptors by providing 360° coverage. The Pechora-type bi-static phased-array early warning radar will supplement the eleven Hen House 1950s-era radars, possibly in breach of the 1972 ABM Treaty. Deployment began during the late 1970s at seven sites: Pechora; Lyaki; Mishelevks; Olenegorsk; Sary Shagan; Kamchatka; and Abalakova. The Abalakova radar is quite controversial in that it is situated in the Krasnoyarsk region which is hundreds of kilometres inland of the Soviet border. This deployment is not consistent with the 'oriented outward' and 'at the periphery' stipulations of the ABM Treaty for early warning radars. The Soviets claim the Abalakova radar is for space tracking, but the Americans charge that it could be dedicated to ASAT and BMD applications. Recent American inspections of the site indicate construction is incomplete and of an apparent poor quality. Three other new Pechora-type radars are being constructed on the western periphery of the Soviet Union at Mukachevo, Baranovichi, and Skrunda. These will result in a complete 360° coverage of the entire nation with modern phased-array radar technology (which is perhaps not up to American standards), and could provide a basis for a national BMD system. These systems are thought to have a 'over-the-horizon' capability that can discriminate incoming RVs thousands of kilometres away in space. By employing 'obsolete' vacuum-tube technologies, these Soviet phased-array radar systems could be quite resistant to EMP.

8 J. Gotting (1985) 'Space weapons and intelligence systems', *Armed Forces*, June: 225.

9 Anon. (1987) 'Soviets comply with treaty by removing radar, U.S. says', *Reuter*, 26 February.

10 See T. Greenwood (1975) *Making of MIRV: A Study of Defence Decision Making*, Cambridge: Ballinger, pp. 171–7 for a good review of this topic.

11 Anon. (1983) 'Washington roundup', *Aviation Week and Space Technology*, 23 May: 15; Anon. (1983) 'Washington roundup', *Aviation Week and Space Technology*, 14 November: 23; M.L. Urban (1985) 'Red star at arms', *Armed Forces*, June: 236; J.B. Rhinelander (1986) 'U.S. and Soviet

ballistic missile defence programmes', *Space Policy* (May: 138–52; M. Feazel (1986) 'German study encourages development of antitactical ballistic missiles', *Aviation Week and Space Technology*, 7 July: 84.

12 Anon. (1987) 'Border photo suggest Soviet laser lead', *Associated Press*, 20 June.

13 C.A. Robinson, jr (1982) 'GAO pushing accelerated laser programe', *Aviation Week and Space Technology*, 12 April: 19.

14 Anon. (1985) 'Reagan, Gorbachev fail to agree on space-based weapons limits', *Aviation Week and Space Technology*, 25 November: 14–15; Anon. (1986) 'German paper says Soviet rays have blinded U.S. spy satellites', *Reuter*, 25 October. This total would represent approximately three times the number of American laser researchers, but such an estimate is open to the usual methodological criticisms.

15 Anon. (1986) 'Soviet laser could be used to test ballistic defence', *Aviation Week and Space Technology*, 31 March: 16.

16 Anon. (1984) 'Washington roundup', *Aviation Week and Space Technology*, 9 July: 13.

17 Anon. (1981) 'Improvements for early warning satellites set', *Aviation Week and Space Technology*, 16 February: 18–19.

18 Rhinelander (1986) 'U.S. and Soviet ballistic missile defence programmes', p. 146.

19 G.H. Stine (1981) *Confrontation in Space*, Englewood Cliffs, NJ: Prentice-Hall, 117.

20 C.A. Robinson, jr (1984) 'U.S. realigns program on ballistic missile defence', *Aviation Week and Space Technology*, 23 January: 24.

21 Anon. (1985) 'Misgivings over SDI', *Armed Forces*, June: 205.

22 Anon. (1986) 'Situation report: Warsaw Pact', *JRUSI News Brief*, June: 2.

23 Anon. (1986) 'Laser weapon lab's destruction confirmed', *Reuter*, 22 August.

24 Anon. (1982) 'Intelligence estimate revealed unintentionally', *Aviation Week and Space Technology*, 6 March: 272.

25 Anon. (1982) 'In sight: killer lasers', *Time*, 15 March: 18.

26 C.A. Robinson, jr (1984) 'Soviets making gains in air defence', *Aviation Week and Space Technology*, 2 April: 23.

27 T.B. Taylor (1987) 'Third-generation nuclear weapons', *Scientific American*, April: 30–9.

28 C.A. Robinson, jr (1981) 'Soviet Union defensive buildup detailed by Weinberger', *Aviation Week and Space Technology*, 5 October: 22; R.R. Ropelewski (1985) 'Soviet high-energy laser program moves into prototype weapon stage', *Aviation Week and Space Technology*, 15 April: 43–6; R.G. O'Lone (1985) 'North Atlantic Assembly declares support for SDI after lobbying effort', *Aviation Week and Space Technology*, 21 October: 20.

29 D. MacKenzie (1985) 'Scientists puzzled as Thatcher backs Star Wars', *New Scientist*, 28 February: 3–4.

30 C.A. Robinson, jr (1978) 'U.S. pushes development of beam weapons', *Aviation Week and Space Technology*, 2 October: 15.

31 P.J. Klass (1986) 'Neutral particle beams show potential for decoy discrimination', *Aviation Week and Space Technology*, 8 December: 49.

32 For some speculations on these occurrences see D. Tonge (1980)

'The "Space Beam" race', *World Press Review*, December: 51; G Benford (1981) 'Zeus in orbit', *OMNI*, September: 53–5 and 115–16; R. Darroch (1982) 'The war in space', *World Press Review*, January: 33; R. Hotz (1982) 'The real Star Wars', *Space World*, August/September: 15.

33 It is hypothesized that a small nuclear explosion is detonated within a network of intense magnetic fields. These fields guide the resulting expanding ball of hot energetic gas, or plasma, through a nozzle and a series of electrical generators. The resulting rush of energy could drive a turbine-like device to produce an intense pulse of electricity that would fire a powerful particle beam to great distances. The entire system has been described as a fusion pulsed MHD generator.

34 For example, see R.L. Garwin (1978) 'Charged-particle beam weapons?', *Bulletin of the Atomic Scientists*, October: 24–7.

35 Stine (1981) *Confrontation in Space*, p. 113.

36 B.L. Thompson (1979) ' "Directed energy" weapons and the strategic balance', *ORBIS*, Fall: 702–3.

37 Anon. (1983) 'Scientific canvas locates innovative defensive ideas', *Aviation Week and Space Technology*, 17 October: 19.

6 SPACE OPERATIONS

1 C.S. Sheldon II (1968) *Review of the Soviet Space Program*, New York: McGraw-Hill, pp. 5–7; US Library of Congress, *Soviet Space Programs: 1976–80, Part One*, pp. 79–90; R Turnill (1984) *Jane's Spaceflight Directory*, London: Jane's Publishing, p. 270. The alphabetical designation for Soviet launch vehicles was developed by the late Dr C.S. Sheldon II, and are in common analytical use today. The American military uses an 'SL' designation for Soviet launchers.

2 Anon. (1987) 'International launch vehicles', *Aviation Week and Space Technology*, 9 March: 158–9.

3 T.D. Thompson (ed.) (1986) *TRW Space Log*, vol. 22, pp. 47–53.

4 Anon. (1987) 'Soviets offer three boosters for commercial launch services', *Aviation Week and Space Technology*, 12 January: 94–5.

5 For more detailed reviews see: Dr A.C. Durney (1985) 'Proton — an alternative launch system', *Space Policy*, February: 81–3; Parfitt (1986) 'Can the Soviet Proton launch western satellites?', *Interavia* August: 903–5; Anon. (1986) 'Proton proposal', *Space World*, September: 8; Anon. (1986) 'Soviets assign Glavkosmos primary space program role', *Aviation Week and Space Technology*, 13 October: 19; B. Goudge (1987) 'Proton and long march — are they insurable?', *Space*, May-June: 30–7.

6 Goudge (1987) 'Proton and long march — are they insurable?', p. 37.

7 C. Covault (1987) 'Soviet Proton booster fails; reconnaissance satellite explodes', *Aviation Week and Space Technology*, 9 February: 26–7; Anon. (1987) 'Soviet space: second failure of SL-12 booster', *Jane's Defence Weekly*, 30 May: 25.

8 Anon. (1987) 'Soviets resume Proton operations', *Aviation Week and Space Technology*, 18 May: 22.

9 J.M. Lenorovitz (1983) 'Soviets marketing Proton in west', *Aviation*

Week and Space Technology, 20 June: 18–20; J.M. Lenorovitz (1983) 'Inmarsat adds Proton to booster list', *Aviation Week and Space Technology*, 1 August: 16–17; Anon. (1983) 'Soviets provide data to guide Inmarsat in launcher decision', *Aviation Week and Space Technology*, 8 August: 22.

10 Anon. (1986) 'Soviets seek western launch bookings', *Aviation Week and Space Technology*, 20 October: 104.

11 J.M. Lenorovitz (1986) 'Soviets offer commercial leases of Gorizont communications satellites', *Aviation Week and Space Technology*, 8 December: 25.

12 Anon. (1986) 'Aerospace spotlight', *Aerospace America*, May: 1.

13 Thompson (1986) *TRW Spacelog*, pp. 47–53. A number of these missions may have been performed by the new MLV.

14 ibid.

15 ibid.

16 For a complete review of the events leading to the MLV deployment see: C. Covault, (1983) 'Soviets building heavy shuttle', *Aviation Week and Space Technology*, 14 March: 255–9; Anon. (1984) 'Washington roundup', *Aviation Week and Space Technology*, 9 January: 15; Anon. (1984) 'Soviets ready new boosters at Tyuratam', *Aviation Week and Space Technology*, 27 August: 18–21; Anon. (1984) 'Soviets strive to outpace U.S. technology in space', *Aviation Week and Space Technology*, 12 March: 111–13; Anon. (1985) 'Soviets develop heavy boosters amid massive military space buildup', *Aviation Week and Space Technology*, 18 March: 120–1; Anon. (1985) 'Soviet shuttle, heavy booster in serious development trouble', *Aviation Week and Space Technology*, 27 May: 21–2; L. Dorr, jr (1985) 'The Russians are coming?', *Space World*, November: 14–17; C. Covault (1986) 'Soviets set to make big gains in outer space exploration', *Aviation Week and Space Technology*, 10 March: 131–4; Anon. (1986) 'Soviets expected to launch space shuttle by 1987', *Aviation Week and Space Technology*, 31 March: 26–7; C. Covault (1986) 'Soviets begin orbiter tests following engine installation', *Aviation Week and Space Technology*, 14 April: 16–18; Anon. (1987) 'News digest', *Aviation Week and Space Technology*, 23 February: 29; Anon. (1987) 'Soviet Union takes lead in manned space operations', *Aviation Week and Space Technology*, 9 March: 129–32; E. Oberg (1987) 'Soviets take medium booster step', *Aerospace America*, March: 8–11.

17 For an historical perspective see R. Engel (1982) 'Soviet "Super-booster" ready to fly again?', *Interavia*, February: 174–5; W.J. Broad (1985) *Star Warriors*, New York: Simon & Schuster, pp. 134–7.

18 Anon. (1987) 'Soviets launch big booster, step up space services export drive', *Interavia*, July: 694–5.

19 Anon. (1981) 'Soviets continue aggressive space drive', *Aviation Week and Space Technology*, 9 March: 88–9; Anon. (1981) 'Soviet booster advance believed to exceed Saturn 5 capability', *Aviation Week and Space Technology*, 2 November 48–9; Anon. (1982) 'Soviet military programs in space move forward', *Aviation Week and Space Technology*, 8 March: 106; Anon. (1982) 'Soviets outspending U.S. on space by $3–4 Billion', *Aviation Week and Space Technology*, 19 July: 28–9.

20 Anon. (1987) 'Soviets demonstrate flight readiness with firing of heavy-lift booster', *Aviation Week and Space Technology*, 16 March: 20–1.

21 Anon. (1987) 'Energia heavy booster to double as Soviet shuttle

propulsion system', *Aviation Week and Space Technology*, 8 June: 18–19; Anon. (1987) 'Close-up views reveal details of Soviet heavy-lift booster', *Aviation Week and Space Technology*, 8 June: 72–3; N.L. Johnson (1987) 'Soviet space: maiden launch of Energia', *Jane's Defence Weekly*, 27 June: 1,384; J.E. Oberg (1987) 'Soviets tell all(?) about big new launcher', *Aerospace America*, July: 8–9 and 46; Anon. (1987) 'Soviets launch big booster, step up space services export drive', *Interavia*, July: 694–5.

22 Anon. (1987) 'Soviets ready new boosters at Tyuratam', pp. 18–21; Anon. (1987) 'Soviets show Mir module', *Flight International*, 11 July: 47.

23 The US Strategic Defense Initiative Organization (SDIO) is spearheading the American HLV effort, in co-operation with the USAF and NASA. However, at this point it is still conceptual and will not approach operational status until at least the mid-1990s. Its projected payload capability is to be less than half that of Energia's.

24 W. Ley (1962) *Satellites, Rockets and Outer Space*, New York: Signet Science Library, pp. 37–9.

25 M.N. Golovine (1962) *Conflict in Space*, New York: St Martin's Press, pp. 55 and 92; E. Bergaust (1968) *The Russians in Space*, New York: G.P. Putnam's Sons, pp. 17–18. Golovine referred to the experimental vehicle as the T-4A boost-glide vehicle, while Bergaust described a rocket-powered skip-bomber.

26 V. Suvorov (1984) *Inside the Soviet Army*, London: Granada, p. 157.

27 P.N. James (1974) *Soviet Conquest from Space*, New York: Arlington House, pp.1 25–42; Lieutenant Colonel C.A. Forbrich, jr (1980) 'The Soviet space shuttle programe', *Air University Review*, May-June: 55–62.

28 The Soviet space shuttle has also been variously referred to as the 'Vozdushno-Kosmicheski-Korably' (air-spaceship), the 'Kosmoljot' (space aircraft) and simply 'the Albatros'.

29 C. Covault (1978) 'Soviets developing fly-back launcher', *Aviation Week and Space Technology*, 6 November: 20. A flyback booster would, in essence, be a large hypersonic aircraft that would employ a combination of advanced gas-turbine ('scramjet' or supercombustion ramjet) and rocket-propulsion systems to reach the high speed and altitude required to launch a space shuttle. It would take off and land horizontally like a conventional aircraft, thereby permitting a wide optional range of orbital inclinations for the space shuttle, which would itself land like a conventional aircraft at the end of its mission. An even more advanced concept, a single-stage-to-orbit space-plane, is currently being developed to various degrees by the United States (National Aerospaceplane or 'Orient Express') and western Europe (British Aerospace's 'Hotol' and MBB's 'Sanger'). It is not public knowledge that the Soviets are actually pursuing similar advanced flyback booster or space-plane concepts at this time.

30 C. Copvault (1978) 'Soviets build reusable shuttle', *Aviation Week and Space Technology*, 20 March: 14.

31 C. Covault (1982) 'Soviets orbit shuttle vehicle', *Aviation Week and Space Technology*, 14 June: 18–19; Anon. (1982) 'Soviets test sub-scale shuttle', *Aviation Week and Space Technology*, 21 June: 16–17; Anon. (1982) 'Soviets test unmanned shuttle-type vehicle', *Aviation Week and Space Technology*, 9 August: 24;

32 Anon. (1982) 'Soviet shuttle program integral to orbital station', *Aviation Week and Space Technology*, 1 March: 24.

33 Anon. (1983) 'Soviets launch winged spacecraft', *Aviation Week and Space Technology*, 21 March: 18; Anon. (1983) 'Soviets recover spaceplane in Indian Ocean', *Aviation Week and Space Technology*, 28 March: 15; Anon. (1983) 'Soviets recover spaceplane', *Aviation Week and Space Technology*, 4 April: 17; Anon. (1983) 'Soviet spaceplane shows crew cabin title details', *Aviation Week and Space Technology*, 6 June: 28; Anon. (1984) 'Soviets end winged spacecraft orbital test flight in Black Sea', *Aviation Week and Space Technology*, 2 January: 14; Anon. (1985) 'Soviets fly fourth orbital test of spaceplane vehicle', *Aviation Week and Space Technology*, 7 January: 19.

34 Anon. (1984) 'Soviets ready new boosters at Tyuratam', pp. 18–21.

35 J.E. Oberg (1983) 'The elusive Soviet space plane', *OMNI*, September: 124–9 and 143.

36 C. Covault (1984) 'Spaceplane called a weapons platform', *Aviation Week and Space Technology*, 23 July: 70; Anon. (1985) 'USSR's space shuttle expected to serve multiple military roles', *Aviation Week and Space Technology*, 3 June: 383.

37 It should be noted that while the primary function of the current American space shuttle transportation system is to truck cargo, the USAF is also very interested in developing a quick-reaction space-plane or boost-glide vehicle somewhat similar to the Soviet concept. The European Hermes could have similar capabilities, as could planned Japanese mini-shuttles.

38 C. Covault, 'Soviets building heavy shuttle', *Aviation Week and Space Technology*, 14 March: 255–9.

39 Anon. (1986) 'Soviets expected to launch space shuttle by 1987', *Aviation Week and Space Technology*, 31 March: 26; C. Covault (1986) 'Soviets begin orbiter tests following engine installation', *Aviation Week and Space Technology*, 14 April: 16–18.

40 Anon. (1983) 'Washington roundup', *Aviation Week and Space Technology*, 18 April: 17; C. Covault, 'USSRs reusable orbiter nears approach, landing tests', *Aviation Week and Space Technology*, 3 December; 18–19; Anon. (1985) 'Soviet shuttle, heavy booster in serious development trouble', pp. 21–2.

41 C. Covault (1986) 'Soviets begin orbiter tests following engine installation', *Aviation Week and Space Technology*, 14 April: 16–18.

42 Anon. (1984) 'Aerospace spotlight', *Aerospace America*, July: 1; B.M. Greeley, jr (1985) 'Soviets target U.S. companies, universities for new technologies', *Aviation Week and Space Technology*, 30 September: 86–90; R.N. Perle (1986) 'Technology security, national security, and U.S. competitiveness', *Issues in Science and Technology*, Fall: 108.

43 For examples of these lines of reasoning see: Dorr (1985) 'The Russians are coming?', pp. 16–17; J.E. Oberg (1987) 'Soviet shuttle mysteries', *Aerospace America*, June: 24–8.

44 P. Smolders and M. Cross (1985) 'Myth of the Soviet shuttle', *New Scientist*, 11 April: 6; M.S. Hillyer (1986) 'Cosmonauts have the right stuff, too: A conversation with Vladimir Dzhanibekov', *Space World*, September: 20.

45 Anon. (1987) 'Soviet Union to create space transport system', *Reuter*, 12 June; P. Marsh (1987) 'The next "shuttle" mission may fly from Soviet pad', *The Globe and Mail*, 13 July; Anon. (1987) 'Soviets launch big booster, step up space services export drive', p. 695.

46 B. Jaques (1987) 'From Salyut to Mir: the evolution of Soviet space stations', *Interavia*, January: 69–70.

47 Anon. (1980) 'Crew of Soyuz repairs Salyut', *Aviation Week and Space Technology*, 15 December: 22–3.

48 Anon. (1981) 'Soviets launch new crew to orbiting space station', *Aviation Week and Space Technology*, 30 March: 24.

49 Anon. (1981) 'Soviets press research in manned space flight', *Aviation Week and Space Technology*, 15 June: 56; C. Covault (1981) 'Soviets initiating program on modular space station', *Aviation Week and Space Technology*, 20 June: 22; Anon. (1981) 'Soviets show assembly of space station units', *Aviation Week and Space Technology* 29 June: 21; J. M. Lenorovitz (1981) 'Soviets study long-duration missions', *Aviation Week and Space Technology*, 28 December: 41–3; Anon. (1981) 'Soviets to expand space processing work', *Aviation Week and Space Technology*, 26 October: 68; J.E. Oberg (1982) 'More Soviet space mysteries', *Astronautics and Aeronautics*, February: 20 and 78–9; Anon. (1984) 'Soviet space station will carry own defence', *Aviation Week and Space Technology*, 11 June: 18.

50 Anon. (1982) 'Salyut 7 launched', *Aviation Week and Space Technology*, 26 April: 19; Anon. (1982) 'Progress tanker resupplies Salyut 7', *Aviation Week and Space Technology*, 31 May 16; J.M. Lenorovitz (1982) 'Salyut 7 team begins biological studies', *Aviation Week and Space Technology*, 5 July: 22–3; Anon. (1982) 'Salyut 7 incorporates state-of-art upgrades', *Aviation Week and Space Technology*, 26 July: 26–7.

51 K. Feoktistov (1985) 'Two hundred thirty-seven days in Salyut 7, *Aerospace America*, May: 96–8; J.E. Oberg (1981) 'Soviet spacewalks', *OMNI*, November: 22.

52 Anon. (1982) 'Cosmonauts work outside Salyut 7', *Aviation Week and Space Technology*, 9 August: 21.

53 L. Dorr, jr (1986) 'The salvage of Salyut 7', *Space World*, May: 8–12; Hillyer (1986) 'Cosmonauts have the right stuff, too: a conversation with Vladimir Dzhanibekov', pp. 17–20.

54 Anon. (1986) 'Cosmonauts deploy space structures during recent EVA', *Aviation Week and Space Technology* 2 June: 20 Anon. (1986) 'Très haute couture — what spacemen will be wearing', *New Scientist*, 5 June: 32; Anon. (1986) 'Cosmonauts deploy structure during EVA', *Aviation Week and Space Technology*, 9 June: 24.

55 Anon. (1983) 'Soviets launch module to enlarge Salyut 7', *Aviation Week and Space Technology*, 7 March: 19; Anon. (1983) 'New crew manning Soviet Salyut 7', *Aviation Week and Space Technology*, 4 July: 26; Anon. (1983) 'Soviets identify cosmos as space station's tug', *Aviation Week and Space Technology*, 11 July: Anon. (1983) 'Soviet space station tug fitted with large reentry module', *Aviation Week and Space Technology*, 25 July: 20.

56 Anon. (1985) 'Successful module launch expands Soviet space station', *Aviation Week and Space Technology*, 14 October: 19–20.

57 Anon. (1986) 'Soviets plan to keep Salyut in orbit', *Aviation Week and Space Technology*, 14 July: 142–3.

58 Anon. (1986) 'The genesis of the Soviet space station', *New Scientist*, 27 February: 19; L. Dorr, jr (1986) 'Mir: the shape of things to come?', *Space World*, May: 11; D.J. Gauthier (1986) 'Mir: the beginning of a lower tech but permanent space station?', *Space World*, September: 24–5; A. Chaikin

(1986) 'Life in orbit', *OMNI*, September: 66   71; J.J. Harford (1986) 'Mir today, Mars tomorrow', *Aerospace America*, December: 6–8; T. Furniss (1987) 'Inside Mir', *Space World*, May: 24–5; R. DeMeis (1987) 'Mir: a second Sputnik?', *Aerospace America*, July: 24–7.

59 Anon. (1986) 'Cosmonauts complete transfer between Mir and Salyut 7', *Aviation Week and Space Technology*, 12 May: 28; Anon. (1986) 'Soviet technology displayed in space', *New Scientist*, 15 May 8: 27.

60 C. Covault (1987) 'Soviet long-duration crew activates Mir space station', *Aviation Week and Space Technology*, 16 February: 19–20.

61 J.M. Lenorovitz (1986) 'Soviets prepare for new activity on board Mir space station', *Aviation Week and Space Technology*, 13 October: 18–19; Anon. (1987) New Mir astrophysics module to include European experiments', *Aviation Week and Space Technology*, 21; Anon. (1987) 'Soviets launch astrophysics module to Mir', *Aviation Week and Space Technology*, 6 April: 24; Anon. (1987) 'The rescue of Kvant', *Space*, May–June: 65; J.E. Oberg (1987) 'Kvant docking shows maturity in space operations', *Aerospace America*, June: 9–10.

62 Anon. (1986) 'Ten ESA member nations join Hermes spaceplane program', *Aviation Week and Space Technology*, 8 December: 27; Anon. (1987) 'CNES discusses Hermes-Mir compatibility with Soviets', *Aviation Week and Space Technology*, 11 May 8: 25.

63 Anon. (1987) 'Mir expansion slowed', *Flight International*, 24 October: 35–6.

7 SCIENTIFIC AND INTERPLANETARY EXPLORATION

1 P.P. Chandler (1986) 'U.S.-Soviet Intergovernmental agreement on cooperative space activities: should it be re-established?', *Space Policy*, February: 28–36.

2 Anon. (1986) 'Reagan, Gorbachev endorse cvil space cooperation', *Aviation Week and Space Technology*, 27 October: 20; Anon. (1986) 'Soviet official endorses space cooperation despite SDI', *Aviation Week and Space Technology*, 3 November: 40–1; C. Covault (1986) 'U.S., Soviet negotiations agree to new space cooperation pact', *Aviation Week and Space Technology*, 10 November: 27–8; M.M. Waldrop (1987) 'Soviet space science opens to the west', *Science*, 12 June: 1,427–31.

3 Anon. (1986) 'British-Soviet space pact', *Aviation Week and Space Technology*, 3 November: 41.

4 A. McIlroy (1987) 'NRC scientists build $4.5 M instrument for Soviet space program', *Ottawa Citizen*, 16 September.

5 For specifics see: R. Turnill (1986) *Jane's Spaceflight Directory*, London: Jane's Publishing, pp. 201–04; C. Covault (1980) 'Soviets plan soil sampler landers for Venus flight', *Aviation Week and Space Technology*, 15 December: 90–5; Anon. (1981) 'Venera 13 carries soil sampler', *Aviation Week and Space Technology*, 9 November: 23; Anon. (1982) 'Venera lander transmits data', *Aviation Week and Space Technology*, 8 March: 266–8; W.H. Gregory (1982) 'A Soviet planetary payoff', *Aviation Week and Space Technology* 15 March: 9; Anon. (1982) 'Second landing on Venus samples

lowland region', *Aviation Week and Space Technology*, 15 March: 17; Anon. (1982) 'Venus surface appears like cooled Basalt', *Aviation Week and Space Technology*, (22 March: 24–5; Anon. (1983) 'Venera more limited than U.S. mission', *Aviation Week and Space Technology*, 13 June: 19; Anon. (1986) 'USSR's Venera images reveal surface features of Venus', *Aviation Week and Space Technology*, 31 March: 121.

6 For the history of the Vega mission see: Anon. (1980) 'Soviets revise 1984 Venera unmanned mission', *Aviation Week and Space Technology*, 10 November: 18–19; Anon. (1981) 'Europeans, Soviets plan Halley data exchange', *Aviation Week and Space Technology*, 27 April: 148; Anon. (1981) 'French participation in Soviet Venus/Halley mission modified', *Aviation Week and Space Technology*, 27 April: 152; J.M. Lenorovitz (1981) 'Soviets express interest in joint comet program', *Aviation Week and Space Technology*, 5 October: 64–9; Anon. (1982) 'Two-spacecraft Venus, Halley mission planned', *Aviation Week and Space Technology*, 8 March: 278–9; Anon. (1982) 'Seven nations to contribute to Soviet comet observation', *Aviation Week and Space Technology*, 12 July: 72; L. Kofler and T. Reichhardt (1985) 'Vega: next stop Venus', *Space World*, June: 25–7; Anon. (1986) 'Astrodynamics', *Aerospace America*, December: 68; Anon. (1986) 'Soviet Vega spacecraft returns data from nucleus of Halley's Comet', *Aviation Week and Space Technology*, 10 March: 289; J.M. Lenorovitz (1986) 'Both Soviet Vega spacecraft relay new data from Halley', *Aviation Week and Space Technology*, 17 March: 18–21; R.A. Kerr (ed.) (1986) 'Weather balloons at Venus', *Science*, 21 March: 1,369–425; R.A. Kerr (1986) 'Vega's 1 and 2 visit Halley', *Science*, 31 March: 1,366; Anon. (1986) 'Soviets set up quick-look center for Halley's data return', *Aviation Week and Space Technology*, 31 March: 119.

7 Anon. (1986) 'Vegas may go on to meet an asteroid', *New Scientist*, 20 March: 22; Anon. (1986) 'New Vega flyby', *Aviation Week and Space Technology*, 24 March 18.

8 Anon. (1986) 'Soviet spacecraft design', *Aviation Week and Space Technology*, 17 March: 18; Anon. (1986) 'Vesta mission will explore Mars, asteroids', *Aviation Week and Space Technology*, 27 October: 54.

9 J.M. Lenorovitz (1986) 'Soviet Mars mission will use new modular spacecraft design', *Aviation Week and Space Technology*, 20 October: 97.

10 C. Stoker and C.P. McKay (1983) 'Mission to Mars: the case for a settlement', *Technology Review*, November/December: 27–37; M.D. Lemonick, (1986) 'Mission to Mars', *Science Digest*, March: 23–34 and 84; C. Sagan (1986) 'To Mars', *Aviation Week and Space Technology*, 8 December: 11.

11 P. Pesavento (1987) 'Tsander's dream', *Space World*, May: 28–31; D. Lindley (1987) 'Plans for Mars impress', *Nature*, 4 June: 361; I. Anderson (1987) 'Soviet march to Mars startles the west', *New Scientist*, 4 June: 30; J. Newbauer (1987) 'Soviets: "Join us to Mars?"', *Aerospace America*, July: 6–7; B.A. Smith (1987) 'U.S./Soviet teleconference highlights Mars exploration program objectives', *Aviation Week and Space Technology*, 3 August: 61–3.

12 Anon. (1983) 'Soviets planning 1986 mission to probe Martian moon Phobos', *Aviation Week and Space Technology* 14 November: 30; C. Covault (1985) 'Soviets in Houston reveal new lunar, Mars, asteroid flights',

Aviation Week and Space Technology, 1 April: 18–20; J.M. Lenorovitz, (1986) 'Soviets urge international effort leading to manned Mars mission', *Aviation Week and Space Technology*, 24 March: 76–81; J.M. Lenorovitz (1986) 'Soviets test spectrometric laser system', *Aviation Week and Space Technology*, 16 June: 92–5; J.M. Lenorovitz (1986) 'Soviet Mars mission will use modular spacecraft design', *Aviation Week and Space Technology*, 20 October: 97; J.J. Harford (1986) 'Mir today, Mars tomorrow', *Aerospace America*, December: 6–8; T. Furniss (1987) 'Phobos — the most ambitious mission', *Flight International*, 27 June: 43–5.

13 Anon. (1987) 'NASA to receive Mars/Phobos data', *Aviation Week and Space Technology*, 11 May: 28.

14 J.E. Oberg (1985) 'Racing the Soviets to Mars', *OMNI*, 112–15.

15 C.A. Shifrin (1987) 'Soviets consider possible Mars rover, sample return missions', *Aviation Week and Space Technology*, 23 March: 26–7; C. Joyce (1987) 'Superpowers shake hands for trip to Mars', *New Scientist*, 23 April: 18–19; J.M. Lenorovitz (1987) 'Soviets will use international experts to help plan future science missions', *Aviation Week and Space Technology*, 19 October: 110–11.

16 B.A. Smith (1987) 'U.S./Soviet teleconference highlights Mars exploration program objectives', *Aviation Week and Space Technology*, 3 August: 61–3.

17 Covault (1985) 'Soviets in Houston reveal new lunar, Mars, asteroid flights', p. 18; J.M. Lenorovitz (1986) 'Soviet lunar polar mission to expand scientific data base', *Aviation Week and Space Technology*, 31 March: 118–19.

18 Covault (1986) 'U.S., Soviet negotiators agree on new space cooperation pact', p.l 27.

19 Anon. (1987) 'USSR offers several missions as cooperative space flights', *Aviation Week and Space Technology* 5 October: 27; Anon. (1987) 'Soviets plan 1992 Mars rover', *Flight International*, 24 October: p. 35.

20 For further details see: M.S. Smith (1978) *Life Beyond Earth*, Toronto: Coles Publishing, pp. 33–4 and 101–9; P. Morrison, J. Billingham, and J. Wolfe (1979) *The Search for Extraterrestrial Intelligence*, New York: Dover Publications, pp. 153–67; M.D. Papagiannis (1985) 'Recent progress and future plans on the search for Extraterrestiral intelligence', *Nature*, 14 November: 135–9.

APPENDIX A CHRONOLOGY OF SOVIET SPACE MILESTONES

1 Date(s) refer to launch dates and mission completion unless otherwise specified.

2 'Firsts' refer to world firsts.

Index

For Product Safety Concerns and Information please contact our EU
representative GPSR@taylorandfrancis.com
Taylor & Francis Verlag GmbH, Kaufingerstraße 24, 80331 München, Germany